ONCE WE HAD EVERYTHING

ONCE WE HAD EVERYTHING

Literature in Exile

Edited by
Arvind Gigoo
Siddhartha Gigoo
Adarsh Ajit

Vitasta
LET KNOWLEDGE SPREAD

Published by
Renu Kaul Verma
Vitasta Publishing Pvt Ltd
2/15, Ansari Road, Daryaganj
New Delhi-110 002
info@vitastapublishing.com

ISBN 978-93-86473-45-5

First Edition 2019
Reprint 2020
MRP ₹399

Editor: Veena Batra
Cover and layout by Somesh Kumar Mishra
Printed by Vikas Computer and Printers

Contents

For Pandit Birbal Dhar and Mirza Pandit Dhar who sacrificed their lives to save thousands of Kashmiri Pandits during the Afghan Rule in Kashmir in the 19th century.

In memory of the countless Pandits who perished in exile hoping to return to their homeland, Kashmir.

For the survivor who chooses to testify, it is clear: his duty is to bear witness for the dead *and* for the living. He has no right to deprive future generations of a past that belongs to our collective memory. To forget would be not only dangerous but offensive; to forget the dead would be akin to killing them a second time.

—Elie Wiesel
Preface to *Night*

For us, history had stopped.

—Primo Levi
If This is a Man

...the survivor makes the prolonged and multiple survival of himself possible in descendants.

—Imre Kertész

Preface

THE exodus of Pandits from Kashmir in 1990 remains a blot in the history of modern India. The year 2018 marks the 28th year of their exile. While most Kashmiri Pandits are now settled in different parts of India, several thousands are still languishing in the township for the displaced at Jagti near Nagrota and in other camps in the Jammu province of the J&K state in India. They continue to live as refugees in their own country, still unsure about being able to return safely and peacefully to their homes in Kashmir. Theirs is a life of disenchantment. Their long-cherished desire for a quiet return is still unfulfilled. Even today, they oscillate between despair and hope, and pray for normalcy to return to Kashmir.

Ravaged by three decades of terrorism, militancy and violence, Kashmir continues to be a flashpoint between India and Pakistan. It is witnessing a revival of radicalisation and religious extremism. The displaced and homeless Pandits find themselves caught in a vortex. There has been little progress on their return to and rehabilitation in Kashmir. Their demand for justice has remained unheeded for years. The clamour for keeping Pandits out of Kashmir has grown even louder. They have been forsaken by successive governments and human rights organisations.

They have even been kept out of any meaningful dialogue or consultation. All things that once were theirs—land, culture, heritage, history and home—have been snatched. They have nowhere to go, but they still lay claim to a glorious history, a distinct and illustrious ancestry and a rich cultural heritage, by writing about it.

What kind of a society, a nation are we if we can't even guarantee a safe return of Kashmir's Pandits—an ethnic minority—to their homeland?

Countless Kashmiri Pandits whose voices stand suppressed aren't even in the socio-political discourse of India nowadays. Nobody knows about them and their dignified struggle for basic, simple things of life. How they have lived? What they have gone through? What they have lost? They are the ones who have experienced humanity in its purest form. Despite having lost everything, they have quietly suffered—and nurtured hope. The humanity of such people must be placed before the world so that the generations to come will know the cost these people paid to survive. This book features the stories of some such people.

The young generation of Pandits, born and brought up in exile, is living off an inherited memory. Children born in camps are growing up rootless. What memories will these children inherit and what history will they remember? What will they think of as 'home'? Years from now, these children will discover their roots by reading the stories in this book.

We hope this book will give the readers a glimpse into the condition of the exiled Pandits who still carry the burden of history with them wherever they go. Escape into memory has become a cathartic experience now.

We pray that someday we, the Pandits of Kashmir, will get to reclaim our homeland, Kashmir, and our lost identity. Until then, narrating stories of our individual and collective struggles—who we are, where we have come from, what we lost, what we endured and how we survived—will keep hope aflame in our hearts.

Kashmir is, and will always remain, incomplete without its original inhabitants—the Pandits.

We thank the authors for writing these stories. Special thanks to the translators for translating stories written originally in Hindi, Urdu and Kashmiri. We're immensely indebted to Renu Kaul, Veena Batra and everyone else at Vitasta Publishing for their support and faith. Without their backing, this book would not have been possible.

Arvind Gigoo
Siddhartha Gigoo
Adarsh Ajit
Jammu—New Delhi
November 2018

Introduction

In the winter of 1990, about half a million Pandits, who are the original inhabitants of Kashmir with a chronicled history of 5000 years, were forced to flee their homes in Kashmir and migrate to Jammu and other parts of India because of the persecution they faced after the eruption of Pakistan-sponsored armed insurgency and terrorism. Those who lingered on in Kashmir for various reasons became soft targets for militants and extremists.

The trouble began in the summer of 1989. Anti-Pandit sentiment prevailed everywhere in the Kashmir Valley. The propagandist broadcasts from Pakistan were disturbing. The streets turned bloody. Protests, crackdowns, anti-Pandit slogans, kidnappings and killings took place unabated. Pandits found their names on militant hit lists. Muslims and Pandits stood divided on religious, sectarian and ideological lines. Suspicion, mistrust and betrayals created partition within the society and human relationships lost their meaning. Euphoria and hysteria prevailed in Muslim households; people believed that Kashmir's secession from India and merger with Pakistan was a matter of days. Inside Pandit households, men, women and children battled fear and uncertainty. Conveniently abdicating their responsibilities towards the Pandit minority, the state government and law enforcement agencies failed to prevent the atrocities committed against the Pandits by terrorists and extremist elements. In the wake of killings of many Pandits and the threats received by them, no effort was made to ensure their safety and security in the Kashmir Valley.

After fleeing Kashmir in 1990, thousands of Pandits lost their jobs, businesses, land, houses and belongings. Those whose only livelihood came from farming were the worst affected. Everything they possessed was gone. Their lives were reduced to nothing. Left to fend for themselves, the displaced people were forced to take shelter in puny canvas tents and makeshift tenements unfit for human habitation. These places came to be known as Kashmiri Pandit Migrant Camps. In these camps, there was no access to even basic amenities like healthcare, drinking water, electricity and toilets. The general conditions were unsanitary and unsafe. Women, children and the elderly, in particular, lived on the fringes of life. What they got to experience in the camps is indescribable. Loss of privacy, deterioration of human relationships, subsistence on bare essentials, mental trauma, existential crises, disease, deaths… A sense of insecurity and deprivation, fear, alienation, and apprehensions about the loss of identity invaded the lives of people who struggled to survive. Life was full of wretchedness and misery. Unable to cope with the loss, thousands perished in camps. People saw the end of humanism; they saw heaven turned into hell.

The apathy towards the Pandit community was so deep-rooted in the authorities and the government at that time that the displaced children and students were denied admission in regular schools and colleges in and around the Jammu Province. Sensing that the future of youngsters was at stake, the displaced community appealed to the government to pay attention to the needs of children and students, in particular. As a result, in July 1990, 'camp' schools and colleges were set up. Like the camps accommodating the displaced, the camp schools too were nothing but an assemblage of shabby and ramshackle canvas tents erected on wastelands far from habitation. The entire set up was bereft of basic infrastructure. Imagine a school without classrooms, furniture, a library, a canteen, a toilet and a blackboard! Students sat on tattered tarpaulin sheets while the teachers delivered the lectures. When it rained, they didn't know what to do and where to go. Yet, despite the adversities encountered by the displaced people, education wasn't made to suffer.

After completing matriculation and Class 12, most students went to other parts of India (Delhi, Karnataka, Andhra Pradesh, Maharashtra) to pursue Engineering and technical courses, hoping to be able to secure jobs later so that they would then be able to support their parents. Moved by the sordid state of affairs and the Government's lack of empathy towards the Pandits in the early 90s, Bal Thackeray, the founder of Shiv Sena, instructed engineering colleges in Maharashtra not only to wave off the capitation fee for the displaced Pandit applicants but also to reserve seats for them. It helped hundreds of students, especially those whose parents couldn't afford to pay for their education and other expenses. After all, people had lost everything.

According to a state government report of 2010, 219 Kashmiri Pandits were killed in the region between 1989 and 2004. But according to a survey conducted by Kashmiri Pandit Sangharsh Samiti, 650 were killed between 1989 and 2008. Hundreds of temples and thousands of houses belonging to Pandits were plundered and ravaged during the 90s.

The forced displacement of Pandits from Kashmir in 1990 was of the worst kind in independent India. What's shocking is that the pleas of the displaced people went unheard. A human catastrophe of such magnitude went unnoticed and unmourned by the world.

As years passed, the writers among the displaced and homeless Pandits, in despair and in longing, produced articles, short stories, reportage, poems, plays, essays, novels, memoirs and other writings in English, Hindi, Kashmiri and Urdu. The sole purpose of their writing was to let the world know what they were going through.

The literature thus produced had a clear purpose—to draw the world's attention to a human crisis of unimaginable proportions.

Through these writings, which continue to this day, the displaced Pandits gave vent to their grief, anger and their yearning to return to their homes in Kashmir. For them, writing became a vehicle for nostalgia and for expressing their unfathomable dark anguish. Besides, they give voice to the hundreds of thousands of voiceless Pandits who live miserable, pathetic and depressing lives away from their homes. Feelings of uprootedness and homelessness find full expression in these writings. This way, the Literature in Exile took shape in India for the first time since the independence of the country.

The essays and short stories in this book show how the exiled Pandits of Kashmir are imprisoned in strange and difficult situations. The literature illustrates their dissent, despair and hope.

This book is divided into two sections. Part I: Non-Fiction, features memoirs and personal essays, and Part II: Fiction, features short stories written originally in Hindi, Kashmiri, Urdu and English. Stories written in Hindi, Kashmiri and Urdu have been translated into English especially for this book.

In *We must leave by the fifth of March*, Arvind Gigoo recounts the societal and political changes in downtown Srinagar, Kashmir, before and during the turbulent period (1980s to the present times), paints a disturbing picture of his struggles in exile and sums up with his reflections on the future of Kashmiri Pandits. 'What will happen to the Kashmiri Pandit community, its culture and philosophy and allied things?' he asks.

In *Once we had everything*, Siddhartha Gigoo narrates how, despite the loss of home, the exiled Pandits living in camps and in rented accommodations continue to celebrate *Pann*, the festival which marks the end of deprivation and the beginning of prosperity. 'Those who longed to return are long dead. An entire generation of Hindus was wiped out in camps. What's left is the residue. This residue will cast a long shadow over the history of Kashmir,' he says.

In *Who were they anyway, they might ask one day.* Tej Nath Dhar ruminates on how the centuries-old cultural identity of Kashmiri Pandits, along with the question of their status, stands neglected in the current political discourse. 'If things continue the way they are right now, Pandits will certainly become extinct as a community after some time,' laments the author.

In *Mother and exile*, Dr Subhash Kak traces the journey of his mother from her early childhood and youth in Kashmir, to old age in America and Delhi. He also reflects upon the importance of preserving the rich cultural legacy of the great Hindu saints, poets and scholars of Kashmir. 'In a deeper sense, with my Mother's passing, I felt as if my last link to Kashmir, my motherland, had been severed,' mourns the author, remembering his mother's exodus from Kashmir.

In *The March that never came,* Parmarth Gupta pays a tribute to his mother by memorialising the story of her childhood in Kashmir. 'And I know, even today, somewhere in my mother's heart is a lacerating wait—a longing for the 'March' of homecoming,' says the author.

In *Our days in the conflict zone*, Kundan Lal Chowdhury talks about how leaving Kashmir because of the threats from militants and then living in exile shaped his own writings. He also recounts the socio-political conditions that led to the exodus of Pandits from Kashmir in 1990. 'The Kashmiri Pandits are spoken of in the past tense now,' he laments.

In *Son's whereabouts*, Pushkar Nath Dhar narrates an incident about how a father lost contact with his son after migrating from Kashmir. 'Kashmiri Pandits became refugees in their own country,' says the author.

In *A house, but no home*, Varad Sharma reflects on exile, loss and inherited memories of his ancestral home in Akura, Kashmir. He explores how an inherited memory has become his only connection with Kashmir where he can't return. 'Who will protect us from cultural extinction in exile? Will the generation of younger Pandits be able to become the sentinels of the community?' asks the author.

In *The boy who ran,* Khushboo Mattoo recalls the harrowing times when her grandfather was repeatedly made to flee his home in Kashmir due to various incidents—the Peasant Uprising of 1931, the 1947 raid on Kashmir by Pakistani tribal militias, Pakistan's attack on India in 1965, the communal riots of 1986, and the outbreak of militancy in 1990. 'In the summer of 1991, the militants abducted Bobji. He was detained at a secret place for three days,' narrates the author.

In *The keys to a house not there*, Pratush Koul remembers his first-ever visit to Kashmir to see his parents' house. 'These people were homeless. Once they too had houses. Now, all they were left with were keys to houses that were not there,' he writes.

The village of vacant houses is Seema Bhat's tribute to her village, Haal, where she goes after twenty years as a tourist. 'I long for the beautiful past to return,' says the author.

In *The home I dream of returning to*, Nipa Charagi examines the idea of 'home' by reflecting upon the losses incurred by her, her family and relatives due to their migration from Kashmir. 'The taste and flavour of home is stashed away in a plastic bag in the fridge containing dried vegetables; in the side compartment is a tiny, transparent box of saffron,' she ruminates.

In *Lost window*, Neeraj Santoshi recollects the stories narrated to him by his grandfather. 'I remember looking at the rain one afternoon through the window of my ancestral house in Kashmir. My grandfather, Tathya, was telling me a story about a King who had lost his kingdom,' he recounts.

Examining the literature produced by Pandits in exile, Agnishekhar, in *Literature in exile,* reveals how Pandits, like Jews, wrote about the holocaust-like conditions they faced after being expelled from Kashmir. 'We have sown the seeds of Exile Consciousness Movement in Indian Literature,' asserts the author.

In *Things we left behind*, Kirti Kaul recalls the night of terror that forced her and her family to leave everything—a home, priceless belongings, a way of life—behind and embark on a one-way journey to a place they could never call 'home'. 'The larger question still remained unattended! Where do we go?' asks the author.

Harikrishna Kaul's *Finger* depicts the love-hate relationship between two friends—one a Muslim and the other a Pandit—in conflict-ridden Kashmir. 'My dear brother, outsiders as well as our own people fooled us… I mean… fingered us. Pakistan and India cheated us,' says the protagonist.

In Henna Koul's *The rented house and the flat*, a girl looks at old photographs and sees her past and present come alive and collide. 'We are alone in this old age. We have no one to talk to, no one to share our feelings with,' says a man in a photograph.

In Chandrakanta's *A tale of the Satisar,* Lalli has not forgotten Reshi Pir, Chrar-e-Sharif, Shankaracharya Temple and Tulla Mulla Mandir. The story presents a panoramic view of a joint family that is torn apart due to migration. 'Losing your home is like climbing on to a pyre or lying down in a grave while you are alive. Only someone who has lost a home can appreciate the real meaning of home,' says Lalli.

Moti Lal Kemmu's *A tale of the animals* is an Orwellian allegory set in conflict-ridden Vananchal in which wolves and jackals conspire to evict the meek deer from their caves. 'Leave Vananchal to the jackals. No one will save you,' says an old jackal to the deer.

Maharaj Krishen Santoshi's *Akanandun* (the only son) is a modern day retelling of a nineteenth century folktale in which a couple's only son, who's supposed to be handed over to a Yogi after turning twelve, is killed by militants. 'Your beloved Akanandun has been killed. He will never come back now,' says a woman to the Yogi.

In Autar Krishan Rahbar's *The shadow,* a man who's unable to come to terms with the loss of his home in Kashmir, due to the religious persecution faced by Hindus, talks to his constant companion—his own shadow. 'My tongue was paralysed. I froze. My shadow clung to me,' says the narrator.

In Khema Kaul's *The city of pain*, a man narrates a horrifying experience of going to Kashmir to retrieve his sister's belongings.

'People thought that I was waving to them whereas I was waving at my deserted lifeless house,' says the man.

In Kishni Pandita's *Wedding album*, a woman takes her daughter to Kashmir and discovers that her old wedding album that she had thought was lost forever has been preserved by her old Muslim neighbour. 'First you should see what I have for you and then you must decide whether you would like to take it or not,' the neighbour says to the woman.

Based on a real incident, Shilpa Raina's *The last cry* is a heartrending story of a girl who witnesses the brutal killing of her grandfather on the day the entire family is to leave their home in Kashmir. 'I immediately rushed to the spot and brought him here. I poured some water into his mouth, but he was dead by then,' says the girl's father.

In Monika Ajay Kaul's *The mirage*, a girl tries to understand why her family is being forced to leave Kashmir. 'You must leave tomorrow. Other Pandits from the neighbourhood are leaving too, and we shall see you soon,' says a neighbour to the girl's family.

In Sushant Dhar's *Avenged*, a Pandit boy travels to his old village in Kashmir to mourn the death of the father of his childhood friend—the very friend who once had justified the killing of the Pandit boy's brother. 'They don't kill innocents. They don't kill without reason,' mourns the exile.

In Deepak Budki's *The informers*, militants kill an elderly couple and the newspapers justify the killing by accusing the couple of being informants. 'Do whatever you think is right. But please hurry. We may not have much time left,' the wife says to her husband, sensing the threat to their lives.

In Adarsh Ajit's *The world cup*, a hockey match played between India and Pakistan divides Hindus and Muslims on the lines of religion and nationality. 'Electricity went out. TV was gone. And we did not watch that goal,' says a Pandit man after seeing a Muslim man cut the electric wire to prevent people from watching the match.

In Rajesh Kaul's *The last rites*, a man performs the last rites of a woman who dies after her family abandons her. 'I got an obituary published in the newspapers, hoping that her family would see her photograph and come for the last rites. But no one came,' laments the narrator.

In Rinku Koul's *Father and son*, a man is unable to attend the cremation of his own father. 'We cannot wait for his arrival,' says the son-in-law after getting to know that the dead man's son can't make it to the cremation.

—The Editors

NON-FICTION

Our enemies did not cross the border
They crept through our weakness like ants.
—Nizar Tawfiq Qabbani

We must leave by the fifth of March

Arvind Gigoo

One evening in October/November 1989

ALL bars and wine shops are closed now. Drinkers are upset. Some persons say that the bar in the Tourist Reception Centre is open. I go there one evening. I find all drinkers there. When I leave the bar to go home I keep standing outside the broadcasting centre of Radio Kashmir to hire an auto. None agrees to take me to Safa Kadal. I stop one auto and act a drunken man. I tell the driver, 'You are a coward. You don't help a man who is drunk and wants to go home.' Piyaray Lal Punjabi is laughing at the act. The auto driver agrees to drop me on this side of Safa Kadal. He tells me, 'I fear Safa Kadal. I have heard that it is a very dangerous place.' I assure him that it is not. When the auto passes through Karan Nagar there are no lights in the houses. Darkness prevails.

I ask the driver, 'Why are there no lights in these houses?' He replies, 'These are the houses of Pandits. Some of them have left for Jammu and those who are here don't come out of their houses. They are in terror. Sir, what did the Pandits do to us? They are our brothers.' He thinks I am a Muslim. He drops me near my home.

MY daughter Henna and I are walking by the house of Maulvi Abbas, our neighbour. The house is illuminated. A function! My daughter doesn't walk and doesn't let me walk. She wants to eat something there. I enter and talk to Abbas about it. About ten persons come and attend to my daughter. I say: '*One rista will do.*' They make her sit comfortably in a room. She eats one *rista* and half a kebab. I thank them and we leave. In half-an hour a full big plate containing *wazwan* (Kashmiri cuisine) reaches home.

1967, Hotel Ahdoo's, the Bund, Srinagar, Kashmir

THIS is my favourite haunt. I spend the evenings here. The tea has good flavour. I come here with my girl friends. They are highly cultured girls.

Today I am having tea with my male friends. They are well-read and well-informed. They are talking about politics of Kashmir. One person, who is an engineer, says, 'Kashmir is the best place for guerilla warfare. We have to fight for freedom from India.' Another man Nazir asks me, 'Who will you vote for if there is a referendum in Kashmir?' Hamid answers him. 'He will vote for India. Yours is a foolish question.' Nazir agrees and laughs. Basheer says, 'Kashmir belongs neither to bloody India nor to bloody Pakistan. Kashmir is only ours… I mean of Kashmiris.'

The summer of 1970, University of Kashmir

I have some work in the administrative block. I see a Pandit boy Vinod beating a Muslim boy mercilessly. Other students are watching. Vinod doesn't stop. He is abusing the Muslim boy who has fallen on the ground. Suddenly the Muslim boy sees a part of the holy thread worn by Pandits around Vinod's neck. He shouts: 'Are you a Pandit?' Vinod loses colour and he runs away. The onlookers ask him to come back but he has disappeared.

1972

Bangladesh is a new country. Yousuf shouts at me on the road. He is very angry. In a rage tells me, 'We will destroy India.' The onlookers are watching the scene. Their expression disapproves of his conduct.

1980

A road goes to Zin Mar by the Eid Gah, a ten-minute walk from my home. One day, I see scores of Pandit men, women and children walking on this road and going somewhere. They are talking of a spring and an idol that are there. I also go to that spot. Vermilion has been applied to the idol. Water is gushing out of an opening. Pandits start praying there. Actually when some Muslims saw the water and the idol they contacted some Pandits and told them, 'This is your holy place. Do whatever you want to do here… pray and erect a temple.' The place was about to become a pilgrimage spot when one day Pandits saw that everything had been destroyed and the idol removed.

That was the end of the pilgrimage.

1982

I teach at Sri Pratap College in Srinagar. One day my colleague Ali Mohammad tells me, 'You Pandits have to leave Kashmir some day.' He has wit and humour and abuses everybody out of fun.

1984

I have renovated the first two storeys of my four-storeyed ancestral house. The house looks beautiful now. Two young boys, who respect and love me, come to my place. They are all praise for the rooms and the walls decorated with reproductions of the paintings of world masters. One of the two named Jeelani tells me, 'Sir, ultimately this house will be ours.' I laugh.

School, College and University

WHEN I was in the government high school at Nawa Kadal for ten years I did not know that I was a Pandit. I was not conscious of being a Pandit. The Muslim boys never told anybody that they were Muslims. This feeling did not exist anywhere.

I learnt nothing in school. I don't remember any teacher. Nor do I want to remember any. I was a shy, silent boy. I became an introvert in love with my loneliness. Neither in the family nor outside did anybody ever tell me, 'You are a Pandit boy.' I used to attend and participate in the *hawans* in the Arya Samaj Mandir at Hazuri Bagh every Sunday. My grandfather, an ardent Arya Samaji, used to take me there.

I taught myself many things in Sri Pratap College. There also I was not aware that I was a Pandit; nor did I meet anyone who called himself a Muslim.

I studied English literature in the university. I continued to be shy. One day, some girls came to me and invited me to tea in the cafeteria. I was nervous and shy but I managed in my own way. More girls came and we become friends. They were excellent at spoken English. I went to their homes. I went with them to Pahalgam, Gulmarg and a couple of other places. Pran Nath,

Ashok Vaishnavi, Hamid Anwar, Ravinder Mattoo, Shuja Sultan, Saulat, Lalit, and others were my friends. We never thought they are Muslims and we are Pandits. I fought with my shyness every time. I do it even these days.

Summer, 1989

PEOPLE—Muslims and Pandits—feel uncomfortable. They talk in hushed tones. Nobody knows what the problem is. I don't care. I feel that they are unnecessarily panic-stricken. But somebody (a Muslim) has been killed somewhere. He was a political activist. Why? I have no answer.

In a matador an old Muslim says, 'What is the meaning of all this?' A young man loses his temper and shouts at the old man. The old man keeps quiet.

I still don't understand the importance of the simmering unrest. My family is ignorant like me. They pay no attention to it. I don't comprehend anything. What is going on here? I see a bearded man break and destroy bottles of liquor that he brought from somewhere in a load carrier. I am sitting in the medical shop of Ashraf.

There have been many deaths. Most of my Pandit friends are tense and worried. I ask them not to worry.

The much-loved Laba Kaul's Bar too has been closed. Torn tapestry covering the sofa sets, dirty curtains, cramped space, risky stairs in semi-darkness, two small rooms, walls of no significance, a very small enclosure called 'bathroom' and the gentleman at the counter with the bottles standing with dignity and grace in the shelves behind him constitute the famous 'Laba Kaul'. It is the hub of writers, intellectuals, artists and journalists. One day, I found the painter Husain talking to the Kashmiri artists. They had invited him to the place. You climb down the stairs, walk about ten steps and Marina Bar (my favourite) welcomes you. This bar is quieter than Laba Kaul's. And Mir Paan Walla is there. Actors, filmmakers and other personalities of Bollywood come to him for *paans*, imported cigarettes and cigars. The bars have been closed under the direction of the militants. Posters about it were pasted on the walls and electrical poles of the city. Someone called Noor Khan, through leaflets and word of mouth, warned the owners of the wine shops of dire consequences if they did not close their wine shops. All obeyed instantly.

Evenings became dull, dreary and dismal.

Autumn, 1989

MY son is taking the class 10 annual board examination in Higher Secondary School, Nawa Kadal. The English paper. He asks the supervisor to give him a continuation sheet of paper. The supervisor says, 'Revise your answer paper. I will give you another sheet of paper.' My son goes through some answers. He again asks for the sheet of paper. My son shouts in the classroom. The supervisor doesn't give him the paper. Instead he says to everyone, 'Time is up. Hand over your answer books to me.' My son is sad. The young man narrates the first painful experience of his life. Sharief-ud-Din and Mohi-ud-Din come to my place and shower abuses on the supervisor. Mohi-ud-Din says, 'A communalist!' My son tells me in the evening, 'I lost twenty marks. Grammar! I would have fetched all the twenty.'

December, 1989

PROFESSORS in college are very serious. The old bonhomie is missing. Students in the classrooms are grim. I reach college early and leave early. The 'coffee house intellectuals' aren't seen.

There is a sombre atmosphere all around. I remain confined to my room or spend the time with my neighbours. I lend Salman Rushdie's *The Satanic Verses* to A K Raina to read. It is an extremely difficult book. I am reading *A History of Chinese Philosophy*. Tao baffles me. I want to understand Tao. I read much in order to comprehend Tao. I get the answer and am relieved. 'The Tao that is understood is not the real Tao.' I close the book. Since then I have not bothered about the meaning and significance of Tao. A political situation that is not understood is the real political situation.

I learn that many Pandit families have left for Jammu. Why? I fail to understand.

Wife, son and daughter are in Delhi. I must go there and get them back. I leave for Delhi. Mother and father are in Srinagar.

A day in the January of 1990

I am in Delhi. The newspaper is very disturbing. I read and reread the news.

30 January 1990

Wife, son, daughter and I leave Delhi for Jammu. In Jammu, we go to the Residency Road to stay in a hotel for the day. Zadoo sees us on the road. He tells me, 'Call your parents to this place. Don't go to Kashmir with your children.' I ask him, 'What happened?' He replies, 'Nothing happened. But I can't describe the night between 19 January and 20 January. It was simply horrible.' Moti Lal asks me not to go to Kashmir but call my parents to Jammu. Why?

31 January 1990

We board a bus to Srinagar. We see Pandits coming to Jammu in taxis, trucks and buses. I want to know what has happened.

There is one young Pandit lady in the bus. We reach the Tourist Reception Centre in Srinagar. It is 7 pm and it is raining. The policeman asks us all not to leave the premises. An SRTC bus comes and all the passengers coming from Jammu board this bus. There is one policeman with a rifle in the bus. Security! He asks the passengers the names of the localities they are to go to. We reach Safa Kadal. The driver says that he will not cross the bridge. I request him to cross the bridge and stop the bus there. He doesn't agree. I shout at him. All others are watching the scene. Two passengers request the driver to cross the bridge because it is raining. The driver turns the bus.

Pandits whisper to one another, 'There will be an army crackdown. Run away.'

February, 1990

A Pandit organisation asks JKLF: 'What are we supposed to do in these conditions? Please tell us in ten days.'

There is no reply. One Pandit is killed. Is this the reply? Pandits think about this killing very seriously.

Everybody says, 'We must leave by the fifth of March.'

'When are you leaving?' This is the refrain of Pandit conversation.

There is terror in the mind of all Kashmiri Pandits called Battas.

MUSLIMS think that *azadi* is a question of some days. Green flags are seen everywhere. Songs propagating jihad are played everywhere. Sloganeering doesn't stop. There is fear and trembling in Pandit households.

PANDITS are an Indian element in Kashmir; so they are killed.

I am in a bus that is coming from Pampore where our cousins live. I found Rani very disturbed and confused. When the bus reaches Pantachok the security forces stop it for routine search. All the passengers get down and remain in a queue for frisking. We are asked to walk about twenty steps and board the bus again. When we sit in the bus a Muslim woman tells the driver, 'One boy has remained behind.' The driver is silent. The security personnel have taken the boy. The woman repeats her statement. The driver doesn't answer her.

When I reach home I see my ten-year-old daughter Henna rubbing with a pebble the two letters HM (Hizbul Mujahedeen) written in green on the tin gate of our house. I stop her from doing so. I get a brush and a bottle of green poster colour and correct it.

1970s

PUBLIC Service Commission Office. I enter the room for the interview. The Secretary of Education J N Dhar says loudly, 'This man goes on saying that the members of the Public Service Commission are corrupt.' And then he leaves. Others watch him quietly. I don't know him; he doesn't know me. I am flabbergasted. Why this?

Appeasement!

The Public Service Commission rejects me five times. Islamia College of Commerce and Sciences rejects me. University of Kashmir rejects me. University of Jammu rejects me. The Jammu and Kashmir Bank rejects me twice. Doordarshan doesn't need me. Radio Kashmir rejects me twice. All reject me.

Eleven years!

And by the time I am accepted, I am tired.

1987-1989

I am in Srinagar. I pay a visit to my friend Showkat who is living in Jawahar Nagar. I stay with him for one night. He tells me that he purchased a house from a Pandit some years back. The house is looking extraordinarily beautiful. I am about to leave his house now. He gives me eleven books that belonged to the Pandit owner of the house.

FROM the window of our room my five-year-old daughter Henna is watching how mutton is being cooked by the cooks on the marriage of Ismail's son. She starts weeping and tells Ismail and me that she wants to eat a kebab. Ismail, his sons and the cooks are delighted. They are our neighbours. I take my daughter to their place where they offer her many dishes. She is happy. When Ismail's granddaughters see my daughter Henna from the window of their house they sing the old song: 'Panditani, Panditani, May your hair burn!' Henna weeps every time they do so.

MUSLIMS die at the hands of the security personnel. Pandits die at the hands of militants. When a Pandit is killed a rumour is spread: 'He was an informant.' When militants kill a Muslim the same rumour is spread: 'He was an informant. An identity card was found in his pocket.' Every evening we hear that someone or so many have been killed.

One evening, Fazi, our neighbour, says in very low voice, 'Uma Shori, Uma Shori, don't drink water. Poison has been mixed in it.' There is gloom in the family. Some persons continue to shout from the mosque during the night.

There is firing from many guns in the lane adjacent to our

house. Father sits in the corridor. Daughter Henna rests her hand on his head.

A K Raina is a strange man. He refuses to understand that the conditions have deteriorated and that people are killed every day. He wants saplings of the flower-plants for his garden in front of his house.

May 1990

I am posted at the Government Degree College for Boys, Anantnag. It is about 55 kilometres from Srinagar. In the staff room the teachers greet me. It is a guarded greeting. Professor Nisar, the Principal, tells me, 'Gigoo, you are under orders of transfer to Amar Singh College in Srinagar.' He hands over the relieving order to me and says, 'Your priority should be to save yourself. Good luck to you.' Ghulam Nabi, the peon of the department of English, comes with me and offers me a cup of tea and a cake at a tea shop outside the college.

TAKAI'S family is one of the gentlest in our locality. They are poor but nice and soft spoken. The news reaches that a security personnel has killed the son of Takai. I am devastated. There is terror when the dead body is brought and kept in the compound of the Bandays. Muslims enter the compound and start shouting. One woman shouts, 'May the seeds of Pandits perish!' I dare not move out of my house. When Maulana Farooq is killed the same woman shouts, 'May the seeds of Pandits perish!' The militants have been blackmailing this family since the day the head of the family did not give the car to them when they wanted to shift a wounded man to the hospital.

I am on the way to Eid Gah. Maulana Farooq is to be buried. Five Muslim shopkeepers come to me and say, 'Don't go there. Go home.' I return home.

MY father is running the Imperial Clinical Laboratory at Maharaj Gunj in Srinagar. He is a highly respected man in that locality. Today he has come home with the microscope in his hand. He is perspiring and nervous. He sits, and after drinking water he says, 'All the women asked me to go home. I will not go to the laboratory now.' I have never seen him so tense and terror-stricken.

I ask Hafiz to arrange any kind of transport for us. He says, 'Go home. A matador will come to you in twenty minutes but don't talk to me on the road henceforth.'

A matador driver comes with a young boy. Four young boys enter the courtyard. They shift the beds, the bedding, the trunks, the utensils, etc. from the rooms up to the vehicle. They are very quick. The matador reaches Indira Nagar, a safe locality where my cousin has his own house. The cousin is in Delhi with his family. I find hundreds of Pandits in Indira Nagar. My wife is very tense. We put whatever we are able to lay our hands on in the matador. One almirah of old books belonging to my grandfather remains untouched. I will come some day and salvage these books. These are rare books which my grandfather bought in Italy, Turkey and other countries.

I hand over the key of the gate of the house to Ismail and his wife. Zarina comes to say good-bye. Musa Banday enters the courtyard and is silent. Through the window, the daughter-in-law of a neighbour, Mohi-ud-Din, tells me, 'Forgive us. Go wherever you want to go. May God protect you!' She breaks down.

We reach Indira Nagar and keep the luggage in the cousin's

house. Father is a shattered man. Pandits here talk fearlessly about everything. I want to go to my abandoned house and salvage grandfather's and my own remaining books, my collection of stones, the latticed window blades (that I had purchased), the portrait of my great-grandfather painted by A N Dhar, the books and other things of my son Siddhartha. Nobody allows me to go there. The news of Bazaz's murder in Habba Kadal reaches us.

11 September 1990

FATHER, mother, wife, son, daughter and I board a truck and leave for Udhampur, near Jammu. All the things have been kept in the truck. We reach Udhampur in the evening and enter the two-room lodge which I have already taken on rent. Father doesn't know what to do. Wife has lost her teaching job in Kashmir. She taught at a government-aided, private girls high school there.

In Udhampur, she takes a teaching job in a school and is paid four hundred rupees a month. Mother misses her relatives and father misses his laboratory and friends.

I join the Camp College for the displaced. There are only Pandit students—boys as well as girls—in the classes. We are all frustrated. Nobody is able to reconcile to the new ugly truth.

I hear that one Muslim family living in our neighbourhood in Srinagar has occupied our house.

I hear that the woman sold all the books and other things to a junk dealer.

I hear that somebody has taken over the two rooms of the Imperial Clinical Laboratory.

FATHER writes letters to his friends… shopkeepers near his laboratory. He gets letters from them. One day I find him weeping. I don't tell him anything. In spite of his stoical attitude towards life he is unhappy, uprooted, alienated and miserable in an alien land.

And then one day in the summer of 1994

'WHY did the dog bite Sanju? He has concealed this thing from all of us. A black dog bit him,' father says to me one day.

'Babuji, no. You are mistaken.'

'Where are the seeds? I want the seeds.'

(I get the seeds of the flowers from the shopkeeper for my father. He puts all the seeds at one place in the ground. He is perspiring.)

'I want that white cloak. And I want that wireless.'

I don't wait. I take father to a doctor in the evening who says, 'This is mental degeneration. It could be Alzheimer's.'

Medicines and more medicines which father always hated.

'Who taught you to fly airships? What did you find on the moon? The sun shrank, became a dot and entered into me. I want the watch with the wireless. I have to talk to Saddam. Kakaji took away all my money in crores and the white robe. Where did the doctor get that cigar? Kuwait! Saddam, Saddam, where are you? Get me Salama, the tongawallah. Get me Ghulam Ahmad. Where are they? I owe Sofi five rupees. Who will pay him? I will do that myself. You should also sleep with them. You have my permission. This profession has a good mission. You should join the mission…'

I listen to all this for endless nights and days. My mother, wife and daughter are spectators. I manage patiently.

One day he forgets the way home. I search for him in the town. Around 2:30 am I find him sitting in a corner by the road. He doesn't recognise me. He is violent at home. Injections. He sleeps.

It is 2:10 am. Father enters my room naked. Wife watches the scene in silence. He tells me, 'Come on, we will go for a morning walk.' I say, 'It is night.' He doesn't agree. I engage him in conversation till it is morning. Then I clothe him. Things are very bad.

Some days later...

Father is admitted to the Medical College Hospital. He remains there for eleven days. Bed sores. Can't be cured. Home. One day I try to straighten his earlobe. The earlobe remains in my hand. Tubes and tubes. Injections and medicines. And then death after three years and nine months of pain and trauma. One day mother tells me weeping, 'I am making you pay for each drop of milk...'

I cremate my father. Death is deliverance for him. I inform his Muslim friends in Maharaj Gunj, Srinagar. They feel very sad. I don't know where Habib and Ghulam Ahmad are. When we left, Ghulam Ahmad wept bitterly.

Father was a very simple man without any possessions and money. He loved cleanliness and order and his transistor set. He was addicted to the evening news. Muslims were his best friends. He was comfortable with them.

1998, Udhampur

Pandits massacred at Wandhama. The dance of death. There is a protest in Udhampur. Thousands of Pandits are shouting slogans on the road. My daughter and I are in the procession. One Pandit tells me that I should not have brought my daughter with me. 'Why?' 'Policemen are here.' We block the national highway. A tall man stands and delivers a long lecture. He is all anger against Kashmiri Muslims. He speaks of the coming of Islam, forced conversion and the destruction of temples. All are very attentive. He speaks of the abrogation of Article 370, land-to-tiller act. The lecture continues for more than half an hour. He concludes by warning Kashmiri Muslims: '*Aur main chetawani de raha hoon apnay musalman bhayiun ko...* (And I am warning my Muslim brothers...). R C Kaul is standing towards my right. I look at him. He smiles. The youth throw stones on the vehicles driven by Muslims. I see Surinder Bharati trying to control the unruly mob on the road. In the evening my landlord Balbir tells me, 'I didn't understand why that Pandit called Muslims brothers.' I tell him, 'Let us have a drink.'

THE goods looted from the houses of Pandits are for sale by the road in Khanayar. Some persons have collected manuscripts in Sanskrit, Persian, Sharada and even Arabic. Some others have collected original artefacts. Pandits had hidden them in boxes in the small puja rooms in their houses. When I found some very old newspapers and other things at home I kept them with me. They are safe because I have a tremendous sense of preservation. Some people have collected original paintings and portraits. Where is the portrait of my great-grandfather painted by M N Dhar, who was a portrait artist those days? He was paid five rupees for it. I remember the eyes, the white beard, white turban, long sleeved *pheran* of my ancestor; the holy book on a low desk in front of him, the brown curtain and landscape through the open window.

2002, Udhampur

MY daughter Henna has done MA in English and B Ed from the University of Jammu. We leave for Srinagar for she has to appear in an interview for the post of a school teacher. The venue is: Service Selection Board, Zum Zum, Ram Bagh, Srinagar, Kashmir. Henna enters the room. Many girls are waiting for their turn. A peon sitting in a chair tells them, 'What a girl! She is speaking wonderful.' When she comes out of the interview room she tells me, 'I talked about Chekov and Siddhartha of Herman Hesse and others.' I am sure that she will be appointed.

When the list is out my daughter Henna Gigoo is not there. Father's history is repeated in the daughter. These days she teaches in a school in New Delhi.

2004, Jammu

I purchased a two-room house from a builder. Mother, wife, daughter and I live in it. I don't feel like going to Kashmir.

Elderly Pandits live in Jammu. The youth are scattered throughout the world. Jammu is an 'Old Age Home for Pandits.' I find unhappy and frustrated old Pandits all around. They talk about Kashmir endlessly. Sunstrokes and snakebites have killed thousands. We aren't used to this scorching heat. Pandits have started constructing their own houses. Many have purchased flats in Chandigarh and other places.

2018, Jammu

There are camps for Pandits. In the beginning it was the tents. Then it was the one-room tenements. Horrible! Now it is the one-room tenements in the camps. The largest camp is at Jagti in Nagrota in the Jammu province. The condition of the Pandits living in the camps is bad.

Most of the Pandits have their own houses now. Many are living in the flats in Jammu, Chandigarh, Mumbai, Bengaluru and other places.

We have forgotten about Kashmir. Children born in 1989 and after know nothing about Kashmir. They haven't seen the Kashmiri Muslims, the snow, the gardens, the various tourist places, the famous Tulip Garden, the lakes, the downtown, the old Srinagar city. Most of the Pandit boys and girls can't and don't speak Kashmiri.

The story of Pandits and their migration from Kashmir to the plains and other countries is over. The children of Pandits are working as engineers in multi-national companies. Thousands of boys and girls are working abroad. Old men and old women feel neglected and ignored. A sense of insecurity is writ large on their faces.

What will happen to the Kashmiri Pandit community, its culture and philosophy and allied things? Nobody can predict. This community produced philosophers, aestheticians, artists, etc. in the past. Now the community seems to be on the verge of extinction. Social, cultural and political organisations of Pandits are trying their utmost to save the Pandit community and its culture. Radio Sharda is doing wonderful work in this direction. Time will decide the fate of the Kashmiri Pandits and their identity.

IN Kashmir I was a Kashmiri first and an Indian afterwards. Now I am an Indian first and last.

Once we had everything

Siddhartha Gigoo

Morning, 8 September 2016

New Delhi

MOTHER and Father have come from Jammu to celebrate Vinayak Chorum, known as Pann among the Pandits of Kashmir. On this auspicious day, *roth* (sweet bread) is made and an age-old story is told. The day marks the end of deprivation and the beginning of prosperity. Mother cleans the kitchen, washes the utensils, kneads the dough and makes *roth*. Then, in accordance with the ritual, she does what all Pandit women do. She assembles us in front of a vessel containing the *roth* and recounts a story that has been narrated for generations:

> Once upon a time in a village in Kashmir lived a woman, her husband and their daughter. They made a living by working

> in the households of the rich. One day, while working in a house, the girl saw the women making *roth*. She had never seen such a beautiful sight. When she returned home, she narrated the incident to her parents. Her mother told her about their past. "Once we had everything," said her mother, "we celebrated Pann, too. Then, our fortunes changed and we were left with nothing." Sensing her daughter's despair, the mother went in search of some wheat and condiments. All she was able to collect were five grains of wheat. She ground them, washed them, and made *roth*. She placed the five pieces of *roth* in a basket and covered them. Then she offered a prayer for the good times to return. When she lifted the cover off the basket, the five pieces of *roth* had turned into five gold coins. "You returned to us whatever we had lost," she said to God. "From now on, we shall always observe Pann on this day."

Mother pauses. What happens next? I ask her. If Babi were alive, she would have told us what happens next, Mother says. May we always be happy and flourish. May we always be together!

A day in September 1989

Our house in downtown Srinagar, Kashmir

Morning

Babi, my grandmother, is cleaning the house and making preparations for Pann pooja. The thread she has spun from cotton wool is dangling off her right earlobe and holding the gold dejhor. I am eager to taste the *roth* and listen to Babi's story. She asks me to sit beside her. She begins:

> Once upon a time, in a village not far from here, lived an adventurous little girl with her mother and father. Once when she was collecting walnuts in a forest, a lion descended from a mountain and blocked her way. The girl wasn't scared. Just when the lion was about to pounce on her, she raised her hand and gave him a smack. Stunned at the girl's valour, the lion ran for his life. The girl returned home and narrated the episode about her encounter with a lion to her parents.

Daytime

My grandfather, father, mother, nine-year-old sister and I gather in the kitchen for the ceremony. After the Pann pooja, Babi resumes narrating the story of the family who had lost everything because of bad circumstances. As always, she doesn't finish the story. She ends by offering a prayer. 'May the darkness dispel. May we never get to leave our beautiful house, our beautiful land. May we live and die happily here. May our descendants flourish.'

Elsewhere in the valley, women across 50,000 Pandit households narrate the same story and offer the same prayer.

Evening

Some of our belongings are lying next to tin trunks. Utensils… bedding. Babi is preparing for the inevitable. Shamboo Nath, our neighbour, has sent his granddaughters to Jammu. Pandit families murmur about fleeing. We shouldn't leave yet, one Pandit says. We will be killed if we stay, says another. Did you hear what militants did to Niranjan's son? They won't spare us if we don't listen to their demands. Ismail and his two sons are dumping arms into a pit in their courtyard. These arms will be used against us. This is a signal for us to leave.

Father decides to linger on for some more days. The very thought of leaving home is unsettling. May we never be thrown out of our home, Babi prays. She tells the story of the brave little girl over and over again. I know who the little girl in the story is. Fear has forced its way into our house. Outside, a frightful night reigns. In spring, Kashmir will become part of Pakistan, a Muslim neighbour repeats. What will you do that day?

The clamour for the ouster of Pandits becomes louder through the ensuing night.

A day in January 1990

Babi visits the shrine of the great mystic, Reshi Peer, at Ali

Kadal and the Roopa Bhawani temple, the birthplace of Roopa Bhawani, the 17th century saint-poetess of Kashmir, and offers a *niyaz* (offering) for continuity and fortitude. At Ishbar, Swami Lakshmanjoo's ashram, she seeks solace.

A day in September 1996, Udhampur, Jammu Province

Morning

I am visiting my parents during my semester break. Grandfather is holding a pack of playing cards and trying to arrange the King, the Queen and the Aces in various orders. One moment, he doesn't recognise me. The next moment, he mistakes me for his father. I am your grandson, I say. Which class are you in? he asks. Don't opt for the sciences. Study humanities when you grow up. I am studying Literature at the Jawaharlal Nehru University in Delhi, I say. Jawaharlal is a good man, he says. Sheikh Abdullah and he are great friends. Grandfather goes on and on. Father and I read about Alzheimer's. Is there any hope? I ask Father.

Daytime

Babi asks us to gather in the kitchen. After performing the pooja, she recounts a story different from all stories she has narrated on previous occasions. We are in Tulmul, she begins. It is springtime and everything is bourgeoning. Temple bells are pealing. Children are swimming in the *naag* (pond). Jigri comes running. Devi has given birth, she says. What shall we name the newborn? Evening falls. Jigri is still undecided. Ninety-seven thousand, seven hundred and seventy-seven names aren't good enough for Devi's newborn calf… After finishing the story, Babi offers a wish. May the darkness dispel! May we never get to leave our beautiful house, our beautiful land!

Babi pauses. We sit still. She begins again: May we return home soon. May we live and die there. May our descendants live happily and never be forced to leave again. Till then, may we remain together!

Evening

I go to the migrant camp nearby. Six hundred families are huddled inside the tents. The women have finished telling the story to their families. Had it not been for the story, they would have perished out of despair. The story has kept them going through the dark times. It has kept hope alive.

Dawn

Grandfather doesn't wake up on time. He has been an early riser ever since his youth. A mysterious smile is playing on his lips. Father decides not to wake him up. Let him dream. The happy dream mustn't end, says Father.

A day in September 2016

Jammu

RAGING mobs of Muslim youth pelt stones at transit camps set up in Kashmir for displaced Pandits employed under the Prime Minister's special employment package. About two thousand Pandit youth, whose parents live in migrant camps in Jammu, live in these transit camps. A friend and fellow writer, Pamposh Dhar, working in a Government Department in Srinagar, informs me of his decision to leave Kashmir. For good? I ask him. My worst fears have come true, he says. Militancy has revived. Our camp was attacked by stone-pelters. What next? I ask. I will return home to Jammu, says he, and resume my research. Pamposh's parents live in Jammu in the Buta Nagar Camp for the displaced Pandits. For a decade, they had lived in a one-room tenement.

What kind of a homecoming has the government thrust on us? Once again, we're being forced to leave our homeland. We're the twice-displaced people. Like many other youngsters who spent their early years in squalid camps in Jammu, were later given jobs in Kashmir, and then, because of persecution, forced to leave Kashmir once again and return to the camps. Pamposh, too, dangles between two 'homes'—a long-lost home in Seer, Kashmir, and the one in Jammu where, after the exodus in 1990, he spent his exiled childhood. His has been a life of strange departures and arrivals. In his camp lived a Pandit woman whose relatives were massacred by militants in Wandhama in 1998. She too died last year. Carrying the burden of the martyrdom of her relatives, she had been suffering alone. It is this burden of history that all Kashmiri Pandits will have to live with for the rest of their lives.

A day in October 2016

Mother informs me of the fate of her cousin, Rattan Nath Dhar. Nowhere to go, Uncle Dhar and his paralysed wife have sought refuge in an old age home run by Bee Enn Charitable hospital in Jammu. Their children are residing elsewhere and are waiting to be informed of their parents' final departure.

The question—what will happen to thousands of displaced Pandits who have been languishing in camps and old age homes for a quarter of a century— should haunt the nation. Who in India will help us in our quest for justice? For two and a half decades, we celebrated memory and kept hope alive in our hearts. But are we to accept rootlessness as our natural condition, forever?

The mendacious designs of the secessionists in Kashmir include obstructing our efforts to return. The successive state and central governments have failed and betrayed us. Human rights activists of India have ignored us. But we won't let Kashmir slip off our existence and memory. We will rise and rebel against those who are hell-bent on preventing our homecoming. But our rebellion will be through our writings and activism, not violence and propaganda.

Bhatta Mazar (the graveyard of the Pandits) in Rainawari, Srinagar, still bears testimony to the brutal repression of Pandits by Muslim dynasties that ruled Kashmir in the fourteenth and fifteenth centuries. Ratnipora, a village near Pulwama where, until 1990, twenty Pandit families lived, is now inhabited by a generation of Muslims who have no clue about the Pandits. Laar, a beautiful stream, flows quietly through Ratnipora. The remnants of an ancient temple stand tall among thirty new mosques that have come up over the last twenty-five years. They bear witness to a history that has been erased by the locals.

All efforts for the political resolution of the Kashmir conflict must take into consideration the history and current status of Kashmir's original inhabitants—the Pandits. Their existence predates the history of Kashmir. There can be no resolution without their collective concurrence. Until their *ghar wapsi* happens, India's story will remain incomplete.

I envision a Kashmir where multiculturalism, secularism and syncretism blossom; where Hindus, Muslims, Buddhists, Sikhs, Christians, agnostics and atheists live in harmony.

When we get to return to Kashmir, we shall reclaim and rebuild everything that's been desecrated and destroyed. Our homes. Our temples. Our culture. Islamabad will be called Anantnag once again. Koh-e-Maraan will be Hari Parbat again.

The Kashmiri word *Pann* means thread. The *pann* holding the story of our ancestry, our history and our future has started to wear off. Yet, our part in the story is not over. For centuries, in our ancestral homes in Kashmir, and for the last two and a half decades in migrant camps and rented tenements in Jammu, our grandmothers and mothers have recited the story to us. It is time the world heard our story.

My grandmother's story will remain unfinished so long as it's narrated outside of Kashmir. Will I be able to keep the story alive with the same hope, the same conviction, and the same compassion? My mother thinks I will.

ON 23 October 1992, Imre Kertész, a Hungarian writer of Jewish descent, delivered an address at the University of Vienna on what it meant for a generation to bear the burden of the Holocaust. The lecture titled, *The Holocaust As Culture*, has become a seminal text on Holocaust suffered by the European Jews. Towards the end of the lecture, Kertész asked an important ethical question. Can the Holocaust give rise to values? For Kertész, deportation from his home in Budapest and serving time in a Nazi extermination camp in Germany at the age of fourteen led him to a deeper understanding of his own condition, intellectual as well as spiritual. The crisis led to the awakening of knowledge within him about the human spirit and freedom in times of horror.

Around the same time, in 1992, when Kertész was delivering lectures and writing about the role of the Holocaust in moulding his identity as a writer, we were battling alienation and deprivation near a horrid migrant camp in Udhampur. Two years had passed since our ouster from Kashmir, our homeland for centuries. We had not abandoned hope despite being forced to live impoverished lives in tenements that lacked almost all necessary amenities. From 1990 to 2000, thousands perished because of lack of proper ration, water, medical care and sanitation. All deaths were unnatural and untimely. I remember going through Holocaust-like conditions for the first few years. Hitherto unknown diseases struck down the young and the old.

Years passed. Nobody paid heed to us. A tent kept a homeless family alive in inclement climatic conditions. A tattered tent. Those of us who survived were not meant to survive. We were just fortunate.

Quoting Jean Améry, the Austrian writer who survived internments in Auschwitz and Buchenwald, and later took his own life, Kertész likens the survivor to an accident, requiring justification, although the survivor is, in fact, unjustifiable.

Survival seems unimaginable, but it's the camps that should seem unimaginable, he says.

We are yet to fully examine our condition from a cultural and civilizational perspective. The losses we were made to incur are unimaginable. Yet, there have been gains. Our immeasurable sufferings during the past twenty-five years have led to an immeasurable knowledge about human morality and existence. And, like Kertész says, if we preserve this wealth, it will enrich the consciousness of our future generations who will have nothing but an inherited memory to rely upon for an understanding of their history.

Writers like Jean Améry, Imre Kertész and Tadeusz Borowski help me understand my own condition, including the possibility of return. Of reconciling my past (from the days of glory to the days of persecution and banishment) and preserving my memory to craft my present.

On 19 January 2017, the Government of Jammu and Kashmir adopted a resolution calling for the return and rehabilitation of Kashmiri Hindus who left in 1990. Within hours, the Muslim separatists warned the government against having separate colonies for the Hindus who choose to return. The Hindus can return though, the separatists said.

Thousands of houses belonging to the Hindus have been either destroyed or bought. Places of culture and worship desecrated and dismantled. Where will the Hindus go, should the government and those controlling the political situation in Kashmir want them to return?

Those who longed to return are long dead. An entire generation of Hindus was wiped out in camps. What's left is the residue. This residue will cast a long shadow over the history of Kashmir.

Who were they anyway, they might ask one day

Tej Nath Dhar

IN his book of poems, *Homeland after Eighteen Years*, which is both a record of and a reflection on his forty-eight hour stay in Kashmir in 2008, K L Chowdhury writes, somewhat sadly, that Kashmiri Pandits have already become a forgotten entity:

Wherever you inquire,
the Kashmiri Pandits are spoken of
in past tense here—
they were,
they have been,
they had been.
Who were they, anyway,
they might ask, one day?

One can understand that the absence of Kashmiri Pandits from most of the localities of Srinagar, especially the ones where they used to live in large numbers, makes the local people talk about them in the past tense. In fact, for the ones who were born after 1990, Pandits are actually an unknown entity. When Sridar, the protagonist of Siddhartha Gigoo's novel, *The Garden of Solitude*, revisits his old house after long years, a young girl of the family that now lives in it looks at him inquiringly and asks her mother, 'Who are Pandits, mother?' The sad truth is that even outside the state of Jammu and Kashmir, people no longer talk about the Pandits. In the psyche of an average Indian, the trauma of Pandits' exile and the problems that it created for them are now a thing of the past. I remember distinctly when I told an acquaintance, not too long ago, about what my community had to go through in 1990, and that even now thousands of Pandits were still languishing in makeshift shelters, he cut me short by saying that he had heard something about it, and just moved on. If Pandits are a forgotten lot inside Kashmir, they are a forgotten lot outside Kashmir too.

It is not that Kashmir does not make news these days. In fact, it does all the time, but now we only hear about insurgency, revolt, deaths, discontent of the Muslims, the measures that have been or should have been taken to address their problems. Newspapers carry reports about them and analyses about their issues on a regular basis; photographers adorn the write-ups with splashes of colour. TV channels do not lag too far behind. But the question of Pandits' demand for justice rarely figures in them.

Perhaps the forgetfulness of people about Pandits and their absence from the current political discourse is largely because remembering their plight does not interest anyone; it does not find place in the agendas of political parties and other influential groups. The truth is that it was like that right from the very beginning. When I was forced to flee my home in Srinagar in

1990 because living in the atmosphere of threat and menace had reached intolerable proportions, my friends virtually begged me to go so that they could sleep well. I found very little sympathy outside the state. During my brief stay in the home of a friend in Delhi, I chanced to meet one of his colleagues, who happened to be a teacher in some local college. When my friend introduced me to him as a Kashmiri Pandit, he did not show any sign of concern or sympathy, and told me to enjoy the holiday with my friend. When I imagined myself holidaying in Delhi in the sweltering heat of June, away from the pleasant weather of my lost home, I felt like hitting him. Fortunately, my friend saw my livid face, took me aside and told me how sorry he was for what had happened. I had hardly recovered from this shock when I found New Delhi splashed with posters in which the government was warned to keep their hands off Kashmiri Muslims, which in those days meant Kashmiri militants, who had inundated the valley with their guns. I was horrified that instead of sympathising with me and my plight, people were concerned for my tormentors!

It took me quite a while to understand why my suffering and the loss of my home did not arouse sufficient interest in the people around me. The forced exile of the Pandit community, which should have attracted the attention of people outside the state as a national issue of serious import, was deliberately projected as a partisan issue. Politicians of several hues issued statements that the exodus of Pandits was a conspiracy engineered by Jagmohan, the then governor of Kashmir. It was truly amazing and shocking to find that people could believe that thousands of people left their homes and hearths in the Valley of Kashmir to languish in ragged tents and subhuman conditions only because somebody told them to do so. My amazement turned into horror when at a national seminar in Shimla I heard a senior professor from one of the leading universities of the country say to a group of top academicians that Kashmiri Pandits had been lured to leave their homes to cause embarrassment to their Muslim brethren and they had been promised plots and flats in different parts of India. That the top leaders of the country and so-called intellectuals virtually spoke the language of the Kashmiri militants was the unkindest cut of all. As a fellow sufferer despairingly put it, 'It was like rubbing salt on our wounds.' Though we were virtually on the road, successive governments at the centre refused to accept our plea that we be declared internally displaced people. Instead, the state government designated us 'migrants,' as if we had left our homes on our own to improve our prospects in makeshift tents!

It is very difficult for me recreate the atmosphere of menace and fear which we were forced to contend with, and which eventually forced us to leave our homes. One had to be there to see how difficult it was even to survive. Although an elected government was in power in the state, it was virtually non-functional. For months on end, militants of all kinds dictated the pace of life and work in the Valley. *Hartals* (strikes) and civil curfews were the order of the day. A systematic program of selective killing of Pandits was at work; two to three of them had to die every day. With relentless regularity, they were told to leave the Valley or face death. To show how precarious the condition of Pandits was, I reproduce a short scene from my book that was published in 2002:

> The image of my friend Bharat flashed past me. How callously he was done to death for no fault of his! Six young men with guns barged into his home, in the very heart of the city, where the houses look ancient… and called for him. Sensing their blind fury, for such incidents had become quite common by then, his parents tried to slow down the pace of their advancing steps so that Bharat could hide himself, but the intruders were simply unstoppable. They pushed everybody aside, overturned everything in their way—chairs, tables, fans, tins of rice, flour, and other provisions—and thundered, *Hand him over to us! If you don't, everyone here*

> *will die*. One of them put the barrel of his gun on the chest of Bharat's mother. Knowing that they would not leave without him, she and her husband pleaded with them for mercy; wailing and falling at their feet, they begged for the life of their only child. Unmoved, the militants spread out in all directions to search for Bharat and found him in an empty drum where he had tried to hide himself.
>
> Pleased with their catch, they dragged Bharat down the stairs and brought him out on the main road, where all signs of life and activity had vanished. They beat him violently, hurled abuse at him, called him everything they could think of—an informer, a spy, a saboteur, an enemy of the revolution, in short, the most dangerous man alive—and then shot him in his various limbs, to finish him off bit by bit. After every shot, his young body writhed in pain, and his cries echoed all over the place. When he asked for water, he got a kick on his mouth and a torrent of abuse. All this happened in broad daylight, in the middle of a public road, in full view of everyone. People watched from a safe distance, behind closed windows, some with approval and some with horror. When the militants were satisfied that everybody around had been sufficiently terrorized, they shot a final bullet into his heart. And Bharat lay there in a pool of blood, at high noon, with flies swarming around his face in dazed confusion. Nobody dared go near his body, not even his parents, because the militants had decreed that nobody should remove it from there without their permission. The most hopeless feature of the entire scene was that the local police post, fully equipped with armed men, was barely a few hundred feet away.

If things continue the way they are right now, Pandits will certainly become extinct as a community after some time. Its young ones, especially the ones who were born after 1990, think of Kashmir as a place where their parents lived once upon a time. In the process of improving their lives, they are merging fast into larger social identities of the country. Their cultural identity, almost like that of the Sindhis who migrated to Gujarat from Pakistan in 1947, is getting eroded by degrees. The governments at the centre and the state make periodic announcements to indicate that they are concerned about their future as a community, but the measures they advocate are attached with so many strings that they hardly work. Several Pandit organisations are trying to keep their voice afloat, but most of the time they are being marginalised. It looks like the governments at the centre and state are just biding time, for they know that, with the passage of time, the voice of the Pandits will get weakened, and then slowly fade away into oblivion.

Unless the people of India make a concerted effort to keep the Pandit community alive by ensuring that appropriate mechanisms are evolved for providing it a proper place and the right kind of atmosphere in the Valley of Kashmir, it will fade away as a community with distinct cultural markers. As Chowdhury rightly puts it:

Who were they, anyway,
they might ask, one day?
And what a sad day that will be in the history of India!

Mother and exile

Subhash Kak

I

MOTHER was a remarkable person. By the force of her personality she became the exemplar for her children and relatives. She believed in working hard but she did not take herself too seriously. Mostly, she laughed at herself.

Mother was born to Dama Kaul (Karihaloo) and Deva Mali in March 1929. She was the fifth surviving child out of a total of six; one older sibling had suffocated to death under piles of bedding and blankets in the chaos of a family wedding. Her father once ran a successful business but later he fell on hard times. She was sent to a school run by English nuns for just a few years until an older girl ran off with a boy to try her luck in the movies. Mother was pulled out of the school and she spent the rest of her childhood playing with her siblings and cousins in the large family compound.

In winter of 1944, she was married to Ram Nath Kak. She wasn't even fifteen at the time. Marriage of a girl at that age was a norm those days. It was the marriage of two families with somewhat different values. The Kauls (Karihaloos) were a typical professional family devoted to good life, good food, and material success. The Kaks valued austerity and maintained or wished to maintain connection to Sanskrit learning. The two families valued the two complementary and oppositional poles of the Hindu belief system related to the man-in-the-world and the renouncer, which are the worlds of Vishnu and Shiva, respectively.

Mother was able to add energy to the relentless urge of the Kaks to excel. She was fun-loving and she liked visiting places and organising picnics; she also loved to cook and entertain people at home. Her fearlessness and independence of spirit came perhaps from the many years she spent playing in the family compound with older cousins and siblings.

She came to value books and knowledge a great deal and nothing gave her as much pleasure as seeing her children and grandchildren interested in learning. She was proud of the many books her children wrote and was truly pleased when Father's autobiography was published posthumously. Her debut book of poems *Nagar aur Vairagya* (City and Renunciation) appeared when she turned seventy-five.

II

FATHER lost his mother when he was just an infant. His father died when he was about ten. For a few years he hung around in the joint family with the understanding that he was now the adopted son of his youngest uncle, Bayaji (Kishan Lal Kak) and his wife Didda. Bayaji and Didda loved him but when they were not around to speak up for him, his other uncles took him to task for some transgression or the other. After witnessing one of the beatings when visiting Srinagar in summer, his older brother, Babuji (Dina Nath), who had, by this time, become lecturer of philosophy in a college in Kapurthala in Punjab, decided to take him there and put him in school.

Babuji was a Gandhian and a strict disciplinarian who was uninterested in money. Father modelled himself much after him. Babuji's wife, Bibiji, resented the fact that she had to bring up her young brother-in-law and this created tension in the family. Actually, Father was not the only young man that Babuji had decided to raise in his home and these other people were not even relatives. This would happen when a poor boy came to study at Babuji's college in Kapurthala and had no place to stay. Babuji would offer to have the boy live at his home during the period of study.

Father's character was also moulded by his efforts to become a yoga expert. He trained to be a veterinarian in Lahore, and was thereupon appointed a doctor in the Jammu and Kashmir Veterinary Department. His postings, generally of two-year duration, took him to far corners of the State. His serious training in yoga took place in Riasi, a town near Jammu where he lived for two years before getting married. His teacher, Jyoti Prakash Kalia, was a lawyer. He was his landlord too.

Mother and Father saw each other for the first time on the wedding day. Kashmiris had the custom of giving a new name to the girl on her marriage and the elders of the Kak family gave her the name Satyavati; her husband also gave her a new name, Sarojini, which became her official name.

Mother had to adjust to unfamiliar conditions after marriage. The Kak household was a crowded place but she didn't have to stay there for any length of time. A few months after the wedding, Father and Mother went to Kapurthala to see Babuji's family.

During this trip she also got to see her sister Aruna and her husband in Muzaffarabad and her older brother Kashi Nath in Lahore. Babuji treated her like a daughter-in-law, and his daughters, Hem and Asha, became very fond of her. Punjab and its glittering capital Lahore were an entirely new world to Mother. Father gave her books to learn Hindi, Sanskrit, and English. She knew Urdu very well. During their stay outside Kashmir, she learnt to speak Dogri and Punjabi. In Leh, she picked up rudimentary Ladakhi.

This was time most Kashmiris still lived by the cycle of festivals, fasts and celebrations. This cycle kept Mother busy. There was something happening every week with special observances on the full moon, the new moon and other days specified in the almanac. In the month of Magh, which fell in winter, Father and Mother, covered in blankets, would set out at dawn to the temple spring to take a dip and do puja. The family priest would show up at home from time to time to look at the horoscope, and on special days such as birthdays he performed the obligatory rituals.

Some of the most magical memories of my childhood are the nights during Shivaratri at our ancestral home in Srinagar, when half-asleep in the early hours of the morning, we kept vigil chanting *Om Namah Shivaya*. Every Janmashtami, Mother would decorate a swing with the picture of the baby Krishna and we would wait until the stroke of midnight to mark his birth.

bel tai madel vena golaab pamposh das tai
poozai lagas param shivas shivanathas tai
With bel leaves, mint, rose and lilies in my hands
I offer my puja to Param Shiva, Shivanath—Krishna Joo Razdan

Songs and music were a large element of Kashmiri celebrations. At the weddings the formal beginning was marked by a chant called *henzaeset* to the ancient Samavedic meter, which told the story of the wedding of Shiva and Parvati. The ladies touched the forehead of other women guests with the auspicious *isband* (rue seeds) that was then dropped in Kangris where they cracked open in the heat producing the most wonderful fragrance.

III

MOTHER'S first child arrived in October 1944. By the time she was twenty-five, she had five children: Avinash, Shakti, Jaishree, Neeraj and me. During the India-Pakistan conflict in 1948-1949, when there was fear that the Hindus of Kashmir would be killed, Babuji persuaded Father and Mother to send Avinash out of Kashmir to Punjab to live with him. Since Babuji didn't have a son, and Mother by that time had two, it was the understanding that Avinash would be adopted. During those times, such adoptions within the larger family were quite common. But Babuji was soon to learn that Bibiji was totally opposed to the idea and Avinash made his unhappiness so clear that after a few years he returned home.

Around the time Neeraj was born, the Government of India was beginning to push the concept of family planning. Mother liked the idea but she couldn't get Father to discuss it. So she took the matter in her own hands and, with the ten-year-old Avinash in tow, approached a lady doctor, a relative who was the director of a hospital in Srinagar to perform tubal ligature. Father heard of it only when she returned from Srinagar.

Mother's heart was full of generosity and goodness. She protected us with fierce energy when we were young, and as we grew older her prayers became our shield.

Perhaps the greatest contribution to her development was the atmosphere of spirituality at home. Father and she met many yogis and saints and that had great impact on her character. At times, she complained of Father's unworldly ways. But she was clearly impressed with his nonchalance and absolute faith in the goodness of people.

Given Mother's keen intelligence and energy that called for

new responsibilities and challenges, she was engaged in many ways with the extended relationships on both sides of the family. She lost her mother in 1950 and father in 1952. For years, Father moved from one small town to another in Jammu and Kashmir State. His postings took them to Jammu City, Billawar and Udhampur near Jammu, Kulgam and Baramulla in Kashmir, and Ladakh. After this, they had an extended stay of six years in Anantnag, and thereupon postings at Chashma Shahi near the Dal Lake and in Srinagar. His last posting was in Jammu. After he retired from the veterinary service, he worked on a part-time basis with the State Bank of India for two years.

Whenever we travelled to Srinagar, we stayed with Mother's elder brother, Radha Krishan, and his wife, Shanta.

Thereafter, we lived in Leh for two years. The winters were extremely cold. We played cards and read books when there was nothing else to do. There was no heating in the house and we would huddle together for warmth. Once Mother had excruciating pain in her teeth. Leh had no trained dentist and the unqualified person who was called pulled out Mother's molars without anesthesia.

In winter, Mother would sit for hours knitting sweaters or socks and humming abstract tunes that were so comforting that one still aches to hear them again. She couldn't sing but her humming was magical.

Daily, both morning and evening she went through the routine of Sanskrit *stotras* that she had learnt from Father. She also recited Hindi and Kashmiri bhajans, and at the end of the puja she sat in front of the pictures of the Gods and Goddesses for a long time. This routine was a discipline that gave her strength. She followed this routine no matter what, even when she was ill. Father's favourite *stotra* was the one by Sakara to Goddess Bhavani:

na tāto na mātā na bhandur na dātā
na putro na putrī na bhtyo na bhartā
na jāyā na vidyā na vttir mamaiva
gatis tvam gatis tvam tvamekā bhavānī
Neither father, nor mother, nor relative, nor benefactor
Nor son, nor daughter, nor servant, nor husband
Nor wife, nor knowledge, nor my work
You are the refuge, you alone are my refuge, Mother Bhavani.

The rest of the day was work. Unlike most other women, Mother didn't make the children help her with the chores. With five children and no heating in the house, there was a lot of work to be done. In winter, the water pipes froze and then she had to take the dishes down to the open yard and wash them under the constantly running street tap.

To an outsider, the sense of spiritual devotion in the Kashmiri home would appear astonishing. The worship of one's chosen deity was imbued with great emotion. Entreaties were made to the Goddess for knowledge:

paade kamalan tal ba aisaye karne chaeney astute
hee bhavani kare me vaeni, sedh mukhus dim sarasvat.
I bow at your lotus-shaped feet, Mother Goddess!
Hear my entreaty! Give me the word, give me the knowledge.

IV

THE troublesome incident of 1967 (the agitation by Kashmiri Hindus asking for police intervention to bring a young Hindu girl back to her parents) had a deep impact on Mother. The girl was legally a minor but she had married a Muslim co-worker and, given the history of rioting in Kashmir, the government did not feel that the option of returning her to her family was a viable one. The impasse continued for several months and Mother participated in the demonstrations. Eventually, the community was exhausted and the agitation petered out. Soon after this, Father was transferred to Jammu.

Avinash went to the United States in 1970. Soon after, Mother's other children came to Delhi to study in the newly established Jawaharlal Nehru University. After my marriage to Naumi in 1979, we left for the United States. By the late 70s, four of the five children were in the US. Mother's sister, Aruna, suggested to her that they should also move to Delhi where many of their other relatives had already moved. In 1981, they relocated to Delhi. Over the years, other relatives arrived in Delhi, a process that was hastened when the Islamists forced the expulsion of the Kashmiri Hindus from Kashmir in 1990.

In Delhi, Mother became the secretary of a group of women who wished to build a temple for Goddess Durga. This group was able to raise money and finally a grand temple was constructed. The affairs of the temple were a big responsibility but also provided great satisfaction to Mother.

V

IN 1986, I was in India for a couple of months as an expert for a UNESCO project. I spent a couple of weeks in Srinagar. Father and Mother came along with me and it was great to be with them and visit several places connected with my childhood. They went back to the United States in 1992 and I remember I was with them in Maryland on Father's seventy-fifth birthday. Thereafter, they came to Baton Rouge for a few months, and, as on the previous occasion, I pressed Father to write notes on his life. These were to become his autobiography.

rātas osum lav zan lärith
subahas pravi ketha trävith gom
At night he was with me like a dewdrop on a flower
At the first ray of dawn he fled leaving me alone. —Arnimal

Father passed away in Honolulu on July 8, 1993. Mother and Father had been there for just over a month, having a good time with Jaishree and her son Vajra, when the thunderbolt struck. But for a bad knee due to arthritis, Father had never been ill in his life and Mother was not prepared for it. They had been great friends and they were now enjoying their travels. Mother was sixty-four when she lost her lifelong companion.

A month later, she brought Father's ashes to Delhi. The following month we went to Haridwar to immerse the ashes in the Ganga.

VI

THE following year, in 1994, Mother agreed to go back to Hawaii for six months. She wished to know if living in Hawaii with Jaishree was a realistic option. The obvious negatives were that she did not know English well and Jaishree did not have a large social circle.

Every afternoon she would walk over to the park near Long's pharmacy and sit on a bench and watch people. Sitting there she would phone me. She was very happy there and she loved going to the malls and to the beach. Shakti also visited them from time to time. Mother and daughters had space and time to meditate on several matters of life. Children at some point in their life discover how much they are like their parents.

During the winter holidays, Naumi and I, along with the children, went to Hawaii for a few days. Meanwhile, Shakti had also arrived there to spend the vacations. We went to Maui and drove to the peak of the Haleakala volcano.

Over the next few years, Jaishree took upon herself to translate Lalla's verses and she wrote a couple of books on them. Mother had always loved Lalla and sung her verses when we were children. She was delighted that she could help Jaishree with the translation of obscure Kashmiri words.

katha gai nenglith atha rūzith
kan china tas ben hekan būzith
sankalpan hund kor sanīyas
Struck dumb and with frozen hands
We can hear nothing but him
Our resolves are forgotten
—Krishna Joo Razdan

VII

BACK in Delhi, Mother wanted to live independently in her apartment. What made it possible was that Shakti lived in the same neighbourhood. Between 1993 and 1995, I came to Delhi on several occasions for observances related to Father's death anniversary. In spite of Mother's brave facade, she remained devastated within.

After the six months she spent with Jaishree in Honolulu in 1994-1995, we could not persuade her to return to the United States. Eventually, we hit upon the idea of doing the thread ceremony of all the boys and girls in the family in December 1998 and convinced her that it could not be held without her. After that she was in the United States every year for four to six months until 2007. On these trips her base was Washington, and she took trips to Louisiana, Indiana, and Hawaii. She was in Baton Rouge soon after Hurricane Katrina hit. Her sister Aruna lived nearby with her daughter and son-in-law.

In the summer of 2007, she visited me in Stillwater when Naumi was in Baton Rouge trying to sell our house as I took up a new position in Oklahoma State University. Her lung capacity had gone down by now. Maybe, it was the cumulative effect of years spent in smoke-filled kitchens. During her visit to Stillwater, I took her out for long walks in the morning, hoping to see improvement in her health. She loved her stay in Stillwater and she liked the attention she received from my friends in the community.

One day, she was invited to give a speech at a temple. It was the first and the only public speech she ever gave. It was excellent.

VIII

IN the last five years of her life she had to use oxygenating machines and nebulizers for breathing every day. But she was as hospitable as ever, always ready to make tea or dinner for guests who dropped by. She remained active and was abreast of news and events.

My greatest regret is that I did not spend much time with her during these years—just a few days on each brief trip to India, although I would talk to her quite regularly on phone. I urged her to keep writing poems. I wanted her to finish her autobiography.

On her eighty-first birthday, I was in Delhi to give a lecture at an event. Meanwhile, she lost her sister Aruna in 2008, and brothers Makhan Lal and Radha Krishan in 2010 and 2012 respectively. Mother was very close to Aruna and Radha Krishan.

In June 2012, Mother was admitted to a hospital and diagnosed with pneumonia. I spoke to her on phone in early June before she fell ill, and told her that I had booked a ticket to visit Delhi in August. When she heard my plan, she hesitated and said it would be too late. I said to her that she would be fine, that her first grandchild was to be married in December 2012 and that she was to make grand preparations for the ceremony. She said she was old and it was time for her to go but then she changed the topic.

After some days, we got a call that Mother's condition was serious. Avinash and Neeraj left for Delhi and when they saw Mother in the hospital they became worried. Mother wasn't responding well. When I got to know of her condition, I left for Delhi the next day. I saw Mother at the hospital on July 11. She was hooked to the breathing machine but she was alert and her mind seemed clear. The doctor said that she looked so good that they could discharge her the next day. Avinash, Neeraj, Shakti, Divya and I sat facing her. The nurse asked her to identify all of us. Mother pointed at each one of us correctly.

When I went near her, she looked at me and repeated the first line of Father's favourite Sanskrit hymn: *na tāto na mātā na bandhur na dātā*. This is the hymn we had all sung together, crying, at Father's funeral in Honolulu. She whispered that it was time for her to go. She said other things too but we could not make out the words owing to the oxygen mask that covered her mouth.

The next morning, Mother's condition deteriorated. At 9:30 pm she passed away.

Jaishree and Vajra arrived the next day. The funeral was done on Friday. The next day, we went to Garh Mukteshwar to immerse the ashes in Ganga. It was a bright sunny day. We rented a boat to go to the middle of the river for the immersion. A cloud had gathered in the sky and it began to rain but by the time we came back to the shore the cloud had dispersed and it was sunny again.

I returned to the United States after performing the tenth-day rituals. I felt empty and didn't want to think what it meant to lose my mother. We did not have her protection anymore.

In a deeper sense, with my Mother's passing, I felt as if my last link to Kashmir, my motherland, had been severed.

The March that never came

Parmarth Gupta

MY mother was supposed to have a normal, happy childhood. But she experienced something else during her school days in Kashmir. She was born on 15 April 1974 in Habba Kadal, a small locality by the banks of Jhelum, in Srinagar. In 1978, she started her schooling. Those days, life was full of small joys. Kashmir was paradisiacal.

Living in a joint family was the best part of my mom's childhood. In the joint family, there were twelve children in all. Family bonding happened when the family spent fun-filled and quality time with one another. Children played games and sang songs during power cuts that occurred twice a week. Due to the power-failure, the family members missed watching their favourite TV shows. It was very disappointing for them. In the evenings, my mom would hang out with one of her sisters on the banks of Jhelum. She loved playing there and watching the water flow gently.

Exhilaration bubbled up within her when she started going to primary school. She made lots of friends. Every day, she would wait eagerly for the school to get over so that she could go home and play with her siblings and her neighbourhood friends. The courtyards of the houses were interconnected. Mother and her friends would navigate their way through small openings in the walls. These interconnected areas provided an amazing place to play hide and seek.

While narrating tales of her childhood, my mom mentions the school picnics that took place once a year. As soon as the sun rose on the day of a picnic, she would wake up with excitement in her heart and head to school elatedly after getting ready. The picnics were usually held at famous tourist places in Kashmir. Frequent hiking trips to the Shankracharya temple, a very renowned and revered temple on the top of a small hill overlooking the Dal Lake, remain an unforgettable memory. 'We were so ecstatic and full of curiosity,' my mother says with a glint in her eyes. 'We would assemble in the school compound before embarking on the trek. We would line up and walk to the foot of the hillock. Then we would trek uphill and pray in the temple. Later, we would rest in the shade of various trees, especially the gigantic Chinars at the base of the hill. In the evenings, we would go back to school before returning homes.'

Another fond memory of my mother's childhood is holding a handcrafted wicker basket and accompanying her grandmother to buy vegetables at the nearby market. She still talks of the beauty of the Kashmiri way of life. 'Kashmir is famous for its fantastic handicrafts and embroidery,' she says. 'Beautifully crafted wicker baskets, kangris, and papier-mâché eggs are a delight to look at.'

Mother also enjoyed boating with her family. They would hire a *shikara* and enjoy the rides on the mesmerising Dal Lake. Once or twice a month, she would go to her maternal grandparents' home in Rainawari. It was thrilling to be there among her cousins. Lush green vegetable fields known as Aramwari surrounded the house. The best part about those visits was walking through the fields and plucking vegetables, often inviting a snub from the owner. Mother and her sisters waited anxiously for different festivals so that they could enjoy the rituals associated with them. Although some rituals were quite hard to perform, the kids still derived joy by indulging in their own playful activities. Cowries and conch shells were treasured and kept in secret places in small pouches. On Shivaratri, everyone remained awake the whole night till my grandparents performed the puja. While the dads and granddads performed the rituals and the moms and grandmas prepared scrumptious delicacies, the kids played different games using cowries. During the puja days, dinner was served at midnight.

My mother tells me how much she enjoyed the events and festivities on Janamashtami, one of her favourite festivals. On that auspicious day, children sat by the windows for hours and then lined up on the road waiting for Lord Krishna's *jhanki* (tableau) to pass by so that they could catch a glimpse. Despite being a Hindu, my mom also waited eagerly for Eid so that she could wish her Muslim friends and roam around in the decorated streets. Her visits to the Mughal gardens and lakes remain an inseparable part of her childhood. She misses all that now. Visiting the gardens in autumn was mesmerising. No grass could be seen on the ground. Vibrant rust-coloured and golden leaves covered the ground. My mom loved experiencing the different seasons. She loved the snow and enjoyed shaking it off the boughs of the trees in our courtyard. She loved how spring sent colours flying through the city. She loved the blooming buds that summoned the birds and animals to come out of their hibernation and fill the air with melodious songs once again. Summers paved the way for school picnics and family outings. Mom fondly remembers the visits to the Radio Station in Srinagar where her dad worked. He was an important officer there and occupied a high post. Every time mom or her family set foot in the station, they were treated like VIPs. And that wasn't the best part of their visit. Outside the Radio Station, there was an alluring Chinar tree. In the shade of the tree was a small confectionary store. Eating chocolates, particularly 5 Star, was a real treat for my mom. Buying chocolates those days was quite a big thing.

In 1997, seven years after the exodus of my mother's family from Kashmir, she visited Srinagar and went all the way to see her favourite Chinar tree, but, to her disappointment, the tree wasn't there. It had perhaps been felled for the new constructions that were taking place.

All these beautiful events are a part of my mom's childhood in Kashmir. Life was going on beautifully until militancy started rearing its ugly head in the winter of 1989. The heaven-like place became hell. Fear invaded the lives of adults and children. It all started when terrorists started pelting stones at the school complexes. Children became afraid and panicked. The streets turned bloody. Kashmiri Pandits (Hindus) were forced to flee from the valley. My mom and her family thought that the militants would be caught and that the misery would be over. Despite all this, my mom left for Jammu in December 1989 with her mother and sisters. Mom's dad was already there. Thinking it was a normal vacation, they had carried only one suitcase containing some clothes and necessary provisions. The vacation was scheduled to end in March the following year when the schools would reopen in Kashmir. My mom was excited to meet her classmates and friends. But that March never came. Militancy spread in Kashmir like wildfire and all Kashmiri Pandits were forced to leave their homes and migrate from there. Several innocent people were killed, seriously injured and even tortured. Temples and places linked with Hinduism were ransacked and destroyed. Hundreds of places were blasted with bombs to inflict terror in the hearts and minds of the Pandits. Mercilessly, the militants took over the valley of Kashmir. This was the most miserable and painful time for Kashmiri Pandits. And I know, even today, somewhere in my mother's heart is a lacerating wait—a longing for the 'March' of homecoming.

She is still the girl she was in her childhood. She is still waiting for the day when she can get to meet her school friends. She's waiting to go to her old home and play in the courtyard of her house. She is still waiting to return to her homeland, the Kashmir of her childhood and of her dreams.

My mom's family had carried only a few things to Jammu. Given the situation in Kashmir, they weren't allowed to go back to their house and bring the rest of the belongings. Militants were targeting people who worked in the Government sector. Even those who were in the media were looked at with suspicion. My mother's family decided to forget their household possessions in Kashmir. But their destiny was already written.

My maternal grandfather's best friend was a man named Lassa Kaul. He occupied a high-ranking post in Kashmir and everyone knew him well. When militancy started, due to security reasons, Lassa Kaul had to stay in his office almost the whole time due to the death threats he received. He had sent his wife and children to Delhi for safety. In February 1990, he went to see his parents who were very old and were staying in a different locality in Srinagar. He got into his vehicle with security guards and reached his parents' home. As soon as he set foot on the ground, terrorists shot him pitilessly. His parents heard the sound of gunshots but they were bedridden. Helplessly they cried and wailed. My mom and her family were at a wedding function when they came to know about the incident. They didn't want to break the news to my grandpa because Lassa Kaul was his best friend. So, everyone at the wedding whispered about the matter and later they decided to tell grandpa.

People gathered around him and told him how his friend, Lassa Kaul, was showered with bullets and killed in cold blood. Grandpa cried. He insisted on attending the cremation in Kashmir but the relatives didn't allow him to go. It was because my grandpa was working for the government and was also on the hit list of the militants. But he wouldn't listen. He was as stubborn as a child and decided to go to Kashmir to attend his best friend's cremation. My maternal grandma volunteered to go with him. She didn't want to leave him alone. One of my mom's cousins, who was in his mid-twenties, accompanied them. When they reached their old house in Kashmir, a Muslim man working in a dairy screamed loudly, 'Who is there?' My grandpa, grandma and the cousin were very afraid. Folding their hands, they begged and pleaded, 'It is us. This is our home. We are Kashmiris.' The man let them be. The three stayed in their old house in Habba Kadal. Their Muslim neighbour came up to them and told them about an announcement in the mosque. It was about the arrival of Lassa Kaul's friend. The announcement spelt trouble for my grandpa. The three had to flee Kashmir at midnight.

My mother did the rest of her schooling in Jammu. In 1997, she went to Delhi with her parents and three sisters.

Now, when my mom takes me to Kashmir, it seems preternatural. My favourite festival is *Pann,* which occurs during August-September. All our relatives gather at one house to pray and celebrate together. We hear the story associated with this festival every year and then eat *roth*, a dish made from flour, sugar and ghee. The women prepare it. Another festival my mother talks about is *Gadhbatta*. She celebrates it at her parents' place. It occurs in winters, around the month of December. On this festival, fish and rice are prepared and offered to the Lord of the house. At the end of the puja, a plate full of rice and fish is placed in the attic of the house for the whole night. And miraculously, the next morning, the plate is empty. The Lord of the House comes at night and partakes of the food.

Khichdi Maavas is another interesting festival of ours. It takes place in winter. On this day, my mom makes *khichdi* and a mutton dish. In Kashmir, my grandparents celebrated it the way it is supposed to be celebrated. They would place a bowl of *khichdi* in the snow-covered veranda. At night, a *yaksh* would come from the mountains and eat it.

One more aspect of being a Kashmiri fascinates me. Kashmiri Pandits celebrate two birthdays falling on two different days every year. The dates are decided when you're born. Priests know how to do the calculations and give you the dates every year. On auspicious days such as birthdays, Kashmiri women wear *athor* (ornament). People make turmeric rice and various vegetarian dishes.

Last year, my mother took me to Kashmir. We stayed at her childhood friend's place. It was a reunion of two friends—a Hindu and a Muslim—who had parted in 1990. Although our religions are different, I feel we share the same culture. It's not about the divide between the Muslims and Hindus. It's the menace called terrorism that is responsible for the tragic happenings in Kashmir.

At my mother's friend's place, I played with her daughter who is my age. She hadn't gone to school that day and I asked her the reason for staying away from school. She said a *hartaal* had been declared in the city. What's a *hartaal*? I asked. She said a shutdown had been declared because some Hindus had killed a pig next to a mosque and the Muslims felt that it was a disgrace. She also mentioned she didn't know why they had killed a pig and why it was a disgrace to her community. Co-incidentally, a similar event had taken place in Udhampur around the same time. Some Muslims had killed a cow, considered sacred by Hindus. There was a savage fight between the two communities. I, too, didn't understand why all of this had to happen. My mom said we should rise above the walls of religions and serve humanity. Her friend said the same. They were happy to be reunited after two and a half decades.

Even though I can't even imagine what my mom and her family went through after their ouster from Kashmir, I still pray that the next generation in Kashmir should neither be haunted by the same ghosts nor be forced to suffer the fate my mother and thousands of other Kashmiri Pandits suffered.

Our days in the conflict zone

Kundan Lal Chowdhury

JANUARY 19 1990, was a watershed in the history of Jammu and Kashmir State. It was a turning point because ordinary people were drawn into the conflict in a big way that changed the character, course and discourse of the Kashmir Valley. On that night, when the whole world was asleep, thousands of loud speakers hoisted on mosques through the length and breadth of the valley, boomed Jihad and *aazadi* slogans and war cries, exhorting the masses to come out of their homes and march to the city to capture power in the Valley. They were urged to cleanse the land of Kafirs (unbelievers), to subdue the Pandit women and drive their men out of Kashmir. Ordinary Muslims came out on the roads while the Pandits shrank back in terror, watching from behind their drawn blinds, trembling with fear from the terrorising slogans that pierced their windows and walls. They saw and heard the threats of genocide coming. The slogans were in question-answer pairs. One slogan, in particular, sent shivers down our spines:

Ham kya chahte? (What do we want?)

Aazadi (Freedom)

Yahan kya banega? (What will we have here?)

Pakistan. *Battav rostui, Battnev saan.* (Pakistan. Without Pandit men, with Pandit women.)

It was the acme of religious frenzy, a flagrant exhibition of mass hysteria. In effect, the Pandits, who were being subjected to selective abductions, torture and killings till then, were finally warned by the whole populace of Kashmir, not just the terrorist groups, to quit and leave their women behind.

From the next day, truckloads and busloads of Pandits were seen fleeing their homes in fright, some even barefooted with hardly any belongings—caravans of men, women and children running away from their homes and hearths. But I stuck to my belief that this was a passing phenomenon; that the age-old traditions of tolerance and fraternity between the two communities could not be wiped away by a single stroke; and that sanity would return to Kashmir. I decided to stay on.

I was wrong. A sudden chill had descended in the attitudes of our Muslim colleagues and neighbours, an eerie suspiciousness, even an indefinable alienation, a hangover from the many little confrontations over the years that had left an indelible mark. It was frightening to discover how even little kids in my immediate neighbourhood had acquired a new lexicon—how they spoke freely in the presence of their parents and elders about *tehreek* (freedom movement) and *jihad* (religious crusade), *mujahids* and *ghazis* (freedom fighters and martyrs), *mukhbirs* and *soyats* (informers and moles), *agwa* and *tafteesh* (kidnapping and interrogation), action (the militants' strike) and reaction (the retaliatory police action), Kalashnikovs and grenades and other terrorism-related patter that betrayed full knowledge and understanding of, and even some fascination for, Jihad.

Selective killings continued but I stuck to my station like the boy on the burning deck. My wife, also a professor, and I continued with our work even as ninety per cent Pandit doctors and our relatives had fled, even as we got threatening phone calls and warning letters from Hizb-ul-Mujahedeen, a major terror organisation. We were warned against staying in Kashmir. 'Leave or face dire consequences,' warned the terrorists. We lived under a pall of fear.

Here are some entries from my diary captioned *The Anatomy of Fear*.

3 March 1990

Fear is all-pervasive. The doorbell rings and your heart flutters, a knock at the door and you take positions, a telephone rings and you wonder whether it is another unknown caller threatening you to take flight or face the consequences. If the call is from an acquaintance, you just whisper or talk in monosyllables or in metaphors lest the phone gets connected with others and your conversation betrays you. You take care to speak in generalities or merely discuss the weather. You avoid any unsavoury allusions to the ongoing violence; you do not utter the words, 'militant', 'terrorist' 'Muslim', etc. In short, you weigh your words in your mind before giving them voice, because whatever you talk or think may pass on to the vigilantes.

You look into your letterbox and your hands tremble while scanning the mail lest there is a warrant from the terrorists. When you go out, you open the door of your house with trepidation; you furtively look for any pamphlets or letters pasted outside, proclaiming you a mole or an informer, an enemy agent or a blasphemer. You walk to the nearest mosque to keep a watch on the goings-on. You go through the names written on walls to see if your name figures in the list of offenders. When you enter the hospital, the walls of the corridors and the wards look at you quizzically. For there you find splashed in bold charcoal graffiti, standing out against the white background, the names of the blacklisted Pandit doctors and paramedics who need to be kept under close surveillance for their suspicious activities or who need to be eliminated. The list is revised very often and you shudder to scan it lest your name figures there.

Then a terrible tragedy happened. Rajnath, an anaesthesia technician in Lalla Ded Hospital for Women, was dragged from his home out into the street and shot, while his neighbours, to whom he would render professional services free of charge, looked the other way. When the news came, the Pandit doctors were stunned. But, the Muslim staff—doctors, nurses, technicians, janitors and others—did not even bat an eyelid. Not a whimper, not a word, not a sigh, not a nod even from his friends and colleagues—as if he had never existed. It so shocked and angered my wife that she almost shouted at her colleagues for having done away with even mere pretensions of decency. Were they in such terrible grip of fear of the militants; had they lost all human values, or were they in collusion with the militants—she fumed. But she only met cold, quizzical stares.

THIS is the worst subversion of human feelings, the demise of simple decencies, the hardening of hearts, the terrible grip of fear.

Well, I still stuck to the burning deck, going about my professional duties, unmindful of the entreaties from our near and dear ones to leave Kashmir. But how long can you escape the dragnet that is closing around you? Yes, a dragnet woven by the prejudiced media who were in collusion with the militants. Here is another entry from my diary:

12 March 1990

The valley-based newspapers have turned into instruments of disinformation, weapons of terror, and harbingers of

> tragedy and death. One shudders with fear and seethes with anger at the inflammatory write-ups and the provocative editorials. The news is distorted to suit the palate of the local populace and aimed at inciting them to hatred and violence against innocents. Running at the mercy of the militants, the newspapers sing paeans to the gory achievements of the Mujahids, and mock at the abject failure of the security forces. It is humiliating to go through the blatantly offensive caricaturing of Pandits, and the wild and terrorising proclamations against them. They are painted as scheming villains and saboteurs, enemies of the freedom movement—the *tehreek*. They are blamed for stabbing the Muslims in the back by running away and leaving them to face the army bullets!
>
> This is strange indeed. If we stay on, we are suspect; if we quit, we are betrayers of the 'freedom struggle' of Kashmiris. We feel ensnared; we cannot claim to be a part of the struggle because it is, in essence, an Islamic crusade. We cannot be out of it; in that case we are against it. Should we leave or should we stay on? That is the conundrum.

A front-page ultimatum by the dreaded Hizbul-Mujahedeen (HM) in *Al Safa* on 14 March, warning all non-Muslims to leave the valley within forty-eight hours or face death, cleared any ambivalence in the minds of Pandits who had braved the threats and intimidation. This was the last straw. Even the Muslims developed creeps. My sister phoned me that morning. She was terribly nervous. Her Muslim neighbour had called on her. 'Till now, we persuaded you not to leave. Now, after this ultimatum, who can vouchsafe your security? Even we feel threatened. Please make your decision. It may be for your own good to go away for some time till things cool down here.' He had sounded apologetic but earnest.

Al Safa also carried a stinging eight-column dénouement of the Muslim perceptions of Battas (Kashmiri Pandits) in the form of a write up captioned *Snake in the grass*. The writer had compared Battas to snakes in the grass that have bitten the unwary Muslims at every critical juncture of history. When a highly provocative and poisonous cocktail of lies and fabrications is dished out to the masses not only through the media but also through other channels—in private conversations, in the mosques, in offices and at work places—how long does an ordinary peaceful citizen resist the impulse to rise and strike at the presumed enemy. My sister decided to leave. But I stuck to the burning deck.

Meanwhile, more and more ordinary people were sucked into the cauldron of militancy during the 'cordon and search operations' that were put in place to flush out and catch the terrorists in the wake of the kidnapping and murder of Mushir-ul-Haq, the Vice Chancellor of the University of Kashmir. The searches, no doubt, caused mental anguish, hurt the sensitivities of the ordinary Muslims, and inflamed them even more against the so-called 'Indian occupational forces'. There was no organised plan of searches. The security forces would pick different *mohallas* and localities at random, call all the occupants out and make them wait for hours in a ground while the searches went on. They sometimes dragged people out who resisted, the old and sick were especially miserable, the women felt humiliated.

Abdul Rauf, the son of a childhood friend long since dead, came to see me after a long time during that period. When I joked that he had forgotten me in these difficult times, he replied that his locality was under siege. He was preparing himself to face the CRPF as and when they decided to come for the searches. He had oiled his limbs, he told me. I laughed and asked the reason.

'When they come and try to catch me and rough me up, as they do to the other youth, I will slip through their grip and give them a difficult time!'

'Have there really been any serious violations—physical abuse, molestation, etc.?' I asked him in confidence.

'They run roughshod in the houses and damage property while they make the searches,' he said. 'We have sent our costly items away to posh areas where they generally don't search. There is a lot of heart burning. It has converted more people who were against the *tehreek*.'

So it is a vicious cycle, a monster that breeds more monsters when you try to confront it. Those dealing with the monster have no idea how to tame it—whether to come down hard on it or use kid gloves. The danger of sucking more and more ordinary people into the vortex of conflict looms large in either case.

The most terrible fallout in conflict situations is the erosion of social, cultural and linguistic traditions, and a tangential shift in value systems. That happened in Kashmir. Radio Kashmir and Doordarshan Srinagar were forced to toe the militant line. The employees were terrorised through threatening letters and phone calls. Lassa Kaul, the Director of Doordarshan, was assassinated. The allegedly un-Islamic telecasts were stopped, the Hindi words dropped from its lexicon, all references to Hinduism and to India avoided except in derogatory terms, and the 'heroics' of the militants beamed unabashedly. The telecast started and ended with the traditional Muslim greetings—*As salamu alaikum* and *Khuda Hafiz*. In the process, more and more secular institutions were Islamised.

Islamisation of Kashmir, and a switch over to Pakistani cultural mores, went on at a rapid pace at other levels as well. People were directed to wear wristwatches on the right rather than the left wrist, and reset the time half an hour behind Indian Standard Time to synchronise with Pakistan time. Shopkeepers and business establishments were ordered to observe Fridays as the off days and to work on Sundays. Under an unwritten rule, state government employees worked only the first half on Fridays, the second half being allowed for prayers, after which hardly anyone returned to work. People were encouraged to speak

Urdu rather than the mother tongue Kashmiri, because it was believed that Urdu identifies with Islam and with Pakistan. In the process, Kashmiris were not only losing their identity but also their language. Kashmir was fast losing its multicultural, multi-religious character.

As to the metamorphosis in moral values, the following episode will be a fitting example. A professor in the University of Kashmir and his wife came to see me. His wife, a middle rung bureaucrat, was having fever. Over a cup of tea, after I examined her, our talk centred on the ongoing violence. Surprisingly, she justified all the heinous deeds of the militants including the ransom they collected and the demand for girls. She claimed that the mujahids were freedom fighters; that they never harassed honest citizens; that the ransom they collected was from corrupt and dishonest people who had amassed fortunes. As for coveting the girls and the alleged rapes, she explained citing the physiological and emotional needs of these young warriors who were ready to sacrifice their lives for the revolution. It was a small price to ask for a much larger sacrifice, she felt, and claimed that the reports of forced marriages and rapes were exaggerated and that most of the girls felt privileged to offer themselves for an honourable cause. It was horrifying to hear her shocking views on militants and their methods. But that is how a conflict drags even the best brains into its nasty grip and changes the perceptions of people.

As if to rebut what the lady claimed, the very next day another patient dropped by my clinic with symptoms of anxiety and depression. On questioning, he said that three militants had barged into his home a week earlier. They had asked for a hiding place because the security forces had chased them after they had hurled a grenade on their picket. 'I put them up in my store,' said the man, 'and they asked me to look out for the security men from the eastern window. They asked my wife to keep a watch from the western window. Then they ordered my daughter to get them food to eat. We kept looking out of the windows for nearly two hours. By that time they had committed the most heinous deed. They had pounced upon my daughter like hungry wolves.'

Another example of a precipitous decline in human character in such conflict situations is borne out by another incident. When I fled to Jammu, an old man came to me for treatment of severe phobic disorder and panic attacks. He had also run away from Kashmir to hide from his son, a militant. The son had threatened to kill him so he could claim compensation that the government had announced for the heirs of people killed by militants.

Finally, it was one of my close subordinates, a God-fearing Muslim, if there ever was one, who begged me to 'leave Kashmir, just for some time, to save yourself, and your family.' I decided to leave on 1 May 1990, never to return (except once for just two days to receive an award) in twenty-three years.

So what happened to my life and that of my family?

An ordinary person leaves his roots, leaves his centuries-old heritage, his whole career, his home, his friends, colleagues and relatives, and his very soul behind to wander in the wilderness of exile, and after twenty-eight years, still wandering, wondering when I can return home to a life of safety and security. But, who cares? The ruling elite, the media, the NGOs, the human rights organisations and activists, all have their own agendas, their priorities and their stakes in how they tackle the subject of conflict. Truth remains buried under false rhetoric, under virulent propaganda, under a blanket of fear. The gun rules, fear pervades, the bold and innocent get eliminated, the scheming and vile people seize the initiative, the ordinary people run for their lives. In this man-eats-man world, the meek are left to fend for themselves.

I am not here to touch on the figures and statistics. We have got into the habit of counting the dead as if we were counting walnuts that we used to bring down by pelting stones on the trees when we were children. How many of your community got killed, maimed, orphaned, widowed? How many of my community? It is so tragic. What we are counting in this 'us' and 'them' game is the Kashmiris done to death, the Kashmiris maimed, the Kashmiris left to harvest the sour fruit of an ugly uprising.

But are killing and maiming and disappearances all there is to conflicts? What about the genocidal exculpation of an entire community from its home and habitat? What about the incalculable damage to human values? What about the erosion of cultures? What about the loss of identities? What about beliefs, family breakdowns, social erosions?

Soon after I reached Jammu, the full tragedy of the exodus of a whole community seemed like a large conflagration. I was caught in it before I could set my foot on Jammu soil. The tragedy was monumental—half a million people had been forced to abandon their hearths and homes in Kashmir. They were housed in temple premises, animal sheds, and camps consisting of ramshackle tents and meagre facilities. The ambient temperature soared to 50 degrees Centigrade in summer sending the death toll soaring. Heat strokes alone claimed more than a thousand lives in the first summer of exile.

When the whole community is displaced and thrown into a totally different environment, and under the conditions that prevail in a forced exodus, the physical, mental, moral and spiritual functioning is thrown out of gear. The moral fabric of the people was tearing apart, the family structure had broken down, and the economic, social and administrative support had collapsed. The memories of terror, persecution and violence in the valley were superimposed upon a feeling of being dispossessed and uprooted. The trauma was further compounded by the problems of acclimatisation, lack of basic amenities like drinking water, drainage, and sewerage. In the camps, there was absence of proper lavatory facilities. There was overcrowding and lack of healthcare, joblessness, disease and death. The multitude of these problems conspired with the compromised nutritional standards of the displaced population and snapped the tenuous reserves of body and mind, exploding in myriad manifestations of disease.

A whole community aged prematurely. Common and uncommon diseases, new syndromes and unique and bizarre constellation of signs and symptoms were surfacing, giving rise to a wide array of psychological syndromes and mental and physical disease. Death, natural and unnatural, hounded the community. All ages, both sexes, all segments of the displaced population suffered.

The displaced people suffered at all levels. There was erosion of values and cultural norms. We witnessed the fragmentation and disintegration of families, the loss of hallowed traditions, the loss of our mother tongue, the dilution in the community gene pool, and the degeneration in moral values. Sons who had a house in Jammu denied space to their siblings and parents. Others forced their parents to sell off their properties at throwaway prices back home in Kashmir, seized the money and threw the parents out on the road. Some others went to distant lands in search of fortunes and left their parents at the mercy of strangers.

On either side of the Banihal tunnel and the Pir Panjal range, Kashmiris—Pandits as well as Muslims—are the big losers. We have lost the groundswell of the glorious traditions that we boasted of, the so-called Kashmiriyat, the harmony in diversity, the tolerance and amity that every one envied in us.

When I visited Kashmir for the first time after eighteen years in exile, I found all the old landmarks blotted out, no sign whatever of my acquaintances, relatives and friends, or their homes.

On visiting the sacred shrine of Makdoom Sahib, I was touched by the faith of Muslim devotees flocking there, but pained by the pathetic state of the Ganesha temple nearby—the gods inside 'abandoned and forlorn'. Here is the irony of the situation.

I find many believers here—men women and children—praying, shedding tears, tying knots, their faces lit up in faith. But I fail to understand how one faith can thrive on the damnation of another? How can love for one nourish on the hatred for the other?

On visiting Vicharnag, once the spiritual fountainhead of Kashmiri Pandits, I cried on finding the place in utter ruin. The temples that housed our gods have now become their tomb.

And at Pokhribal, I mused: Who is worse off, I wonder—the gods here sans their flock or the flock in exile sans their gods?

That is how in situations of conflict, ordinary lives may come to question the very basis of faith that has sustained them all through.

Do I sound terribly pessimistic? Is there no hope in this seemingly irretrievable situation of despondency and depression? Can we revive Kashmir? Can we go back to the hallowed past? That is the question we must answer. Even at the very height of the crisis I saw a ray of hope. I see flickers of light now and then. It is not all dark. The question is: Can we turn the situation around?

There have been some daring examples of Pandits returning to their homes, but they are few. In my latest book of short stories *Faith and Frenzy* which is based on true events, the story *The Return of Natives* describes an old Pandit couple returning to their village, Gasi Rana in Kulgam, after eighteen years and being persuaded by the Muslims to stay on and start life anew. The last I know is that the couple came to Jammu to celebrate Shivaratri with their children and grandchildren, only to return to their village with the traditional gift of walnuts for the villagers.

The tragedy of our times is that Kashmiri Pandits are spoken of in the past tense now. Who were they, anyway, you might ask one day?

A lone swallow does not mean summer. But it can be a harbinger. I hope and pray for that summer of Kashmir that thaws the ice of frozen relationships and warms the hearts that crave for each other. It is in that spirit of good will, of rapprochement and of reconciliation that I am here, armed with a strong awareness of shared history, shared culture and shared heritage and with the hope that together we will carve out a common destiny of peace, progress and prosperity for Jammu and Kashmir.

Son's whereabouts

Pushkar Nath Dhar

ELDERS used to say that the entire activity of the valley of Kashmir would come to a halt for six long months once it snowed on the Banihal Road. After the Maharaja abdicated the throne, we got Awami Raj (Rule of People) with independence. Half of Kashmir, including Muzaffarabad, was forcibly annexed by Pakistan. Then the project Jawahar Tunnel was executed. Indian currency started flowing freely. People were awakened. But Kashmiri Pandits became an eyesore for the majority community and they were kept socially and economically backward because they did not form a large vote-bank. Somehow, Kashmiri Hindus survived in the valley for many decades. But it also did not last long as they were forcibly thrown out of the valley in 1990. With hand grenades and Kalashnikovs, the militants started massacres, loot and arson of Hindus. In spite of an elected government at the helm, the Hindus had no choice but to flee. Thus the militants wrote a new chapter in history after the Awami Raj. Kashmiri Pandits became refugees in their own country. They got scattered. They were brought to a pass, which was not witnessed even during the Partition.

Even about fifty years after Independence, a hopeless father didn't know the whereabouts of his son and his family.

A couple had two sons. When they migrated from Kashmir they went straight to London where their younger son worked. After a couple of years' stay they returned to Delhi. All the time they had no information about their elder son. They inquired of all their relatives and erstwhile neighbours of the valley but without any positive response. At last, they brought out a notice in *Koshur Samachar* when the mother fell ill and was hospitalised.

> Dear son,
> I have returned from London, but I don't know anything about you. You were earlier working in Delhi University. But I was informed that you gave up your job three years ago. Your mother is currently admitted in the AIIMS, Delhi. She eagerly awaits you to come and feed her the Ganga water before she gives up her life.
>
> Dear readers,
> If anybody knows my son and his whereabouts, please inform his hopeless father. My son had been appointed a professor in the University of Delhi after getting his PhD He is the son-in-law of Mr.... If he is in Delhi or anywhere else, he should contact me.
> My address is...

Numberless people who read *Koshur Samachar* must have read the notice. Perhaps the mother died without seeing her son. Maybe, the father ultimately found his son and grandchildren. But who offered the sacred Ganga water to the dying woman? No one knows. Long ago, Kashmiri Hindus must have faced the same predicament when, they say, only eleven Pandit families were left in Kashmir. Many writers tried to record that history. Who has the capacity to record the brutalities meted out to Kashmiri Hindus during the 1990 exodus and the loot, arson and abuse they were subjected to in 1931, in order to exterminate this race once and for all?

Circumstances were created in which a father lost contact with his son. I wish another Prem Chand would emerge from amongst us and record our story. There, indeed, will be many writers. But they will write only in English, Urdu or Hindi. Kashmiri language is anathema to them.

Nothing can save you if you are determined to burn your own house. If we leave it to the Kashmiri Pandit fraternity, then silence is golden.

(Translated from Kashmiri by P L Waguzari)

A house, but no home

Varad Sharma

SOME time ago, on a hot summer day, I visited Jagti along with my father. Jagti is a village near Nagrota town in Jammu province, which straddles the national highway connecting Jammu and Srinagar. At present, Jagti gives shelter to around 4,000 displaced Kashmiri Pandit families; seeing the clustered structures, I couldn't fathom how they must live. Families that once lived in large houses in Kashmir now live in small two-room flats.

I spotted an under-construction temple of goddess Kheer Bhawani, the celebrated deity of Kashmiri Pandits. The original temple is in Tulmul, in Ganderbal district, Kashmir. Every year, thousands of Pandits still visit the Kheer Bhawani temple on Jyeshth Ashtami, in accordance with the Kashmiri Hindu calendar. The temple is a symbol of our uncompromising faith, which we clung to even after being rendered homeless.

In the 'migrant township', I was again reminded of my identity—a Pandit, a migrant, a refugee, an exile. One of my grandfather's cousins lives here with his family. Among other things, my father and his relative talked about our house and the neighbours in Akura, a village in Anantnag district. According to legend, when Shiva was going to the Amarnath cave to relay the Amar Katha to Parvati, he told Ganesha to leave his vehicle, Mushak, at a place that came to be known as Akurath (the other name for Mushak). Akurath was distorted to the present name, Akura. In colloquial Kashmiri, our village is called Okur.

Until 1990, before the exodus of Kashmiri Pandits, my grandfather and his family, and this cousin and his family, all lived in the same house there. The larger part belonged to my grandfather. My father tells me that 'Om' and 'Vikrami Samvat 2009' were inscribed above the front door. Built in 1952, it was a typical village dwelling of bricks, wood and mud with tin roofs.

Our house had three storeys. The ground floor was called *wout*, the first one *kuth*, the second one *kaeni* and above it, there was the *braer kaeni*. The two portions of the house were segmented by an entrance hall known as the *wuzz*. There was the *dub*, a covered balcony above the first floor, protruding out of the entire structure.

In the courtyard, there was the *gaan* (the cowshed), on one side and *daan kuth* (a store house for grains), on the other. The whole area was enclosed by a compound wall called *dwous* made of stones and mud, five or six feet high. The gate made of wood was called *baryen*. Outside the house, a brook of the river Lidder flowed.

For me, it is an inherited memory. I often tell my friend Siddhartha Gigoo that at least he has his own memories—I don't have a single one. Having never lived in Kashmir, I survive on inherited and borrowed memories, to which my Kashmiri identity is affixed. Sometimes, I wonder whether it is possible to inherit all the memories from my parents and relatives. I wish they were tangible so I could keep count of them. I fear the loss of memory; I fear the loss of my Kashmiri identity.

My cousin visited Kashmir recently and shared a picture of our home in Akura. He tells me he identified the place without anyone's guidance and was reminded of our uncle and grand-uncle who would take him to the river Lidder nearby. He met our immediate neighbours, who inquired about our whereabouts. Nobody asked him about coming back. The neighbours admitted that when Pandits used to live in Kashmir, their children were disciplined. From the photograph, it seemed like the conflict, the neighbours and time had all taken their toll on our house.

I heard from my father that our farmland was being occupied by one of our neighbours. That person was supposedly my younger uncle's friend. He had sent a message, my father tells me, asking us to sell our land to him. We declined. Then we heard that he had built a school there.

A fellow Kashmiri, a friend, occupies our land and constructs a school. The betrayal that began in 1990 continues. I am told that we, the minority Hindus who were forced into exile in 1990, should move towards reconciliation with Kashmiri Muslims. What should I reconcile with? I fail to understand.

Still, I don't feel any ill-will against the person who occupied our land. Maybe tomorrow someone will take our house too. I have doubts about reconciliation in such circumstances. My heart says that reconciliation is the way forward but my mind says that I am being asinine. My neighbours in Akura should have kept our home and land intact, if they were concerned about us. Betrayals don't lead to reconciliation.

On how many fronts am I, an exile in my own country, supposed to fight? I am fighting the injustice to me and my community, which has struggled to survive for three decades. I am fighting for the right to a home in my own land. I am struggling to preserve a centuries-old culture. I am surviving, too.

There is a walnut tree in our courtyard which was sown by my father's great-grandfather. That walnut tree is testimony to all that happened to my home and my homeland. I wish that tree could speak.

My cousin shared another photograph of himself and his son, who is nearly three, inside the house. Will his generation, the progeny of our community, feel connected with Kashmir at all? If they won't, what will become of us? Are some communities supposed to assimilate with other communities? Are some identities supposed to cease to exist and cultures supposed to vanish? I don't have answers.

Two months ago, my grand-aunt passed away in Jammu. She was the last of the old generation from my grandmother's side of the family. We used to call her Byengash. While her pyre was being lit, a thought struck me. The older guardians of our community are dying. What will happen to the memories that they possess and we don't? Who will protect us from cultural extinction in exile? Will the generation of younger Pandits be able to become the sentinels of the community? I hope they will. The optimist in me won't let me believe otherwise.

I find solace in my favourite Kashmiri poet Dina Nath Nadim's lines:

Wushun wushun, wazul wazul, wazul wazul, wushun wushun
Wushun wazul, wazul wushun chu khoon myon
Jawan chus, toofan hyu junoon myon
(Warm warm, red red, red red, warm warm
Warm red, red warm is my blood
I am young, my zeal is like a storm.)

The boy who ran

Khushboo Mattoo

IT is a beautiful sunny day in the spring of 1931. The snow has started to melt. The winter hasn't been brutal. Radhakrishan is gloomy because, like the winter, he is fond of drama and springing up surprises. His propensity for thrill and adventure worries his mother who just can't cope with his newfound talent of climbing trees. She stops him from stepping out of the house. He tells her that he doesn't like her because she keeps him away from his wanderlust.

Radhakrishan is a six-year-old boy, the youngest and the most pampered amongst Zana Bhat's three grandsons. The little brat loves to loiter in the orchards of his grandfather. He has discovered the joy of being among the trees laden with fruit. Zana Bhat, is the only zamindar at Kanikoot, a small hamlet that is a few kilometres uphill from Naigam in the Chadoora tehsil of Budgam in Kashmir.

Zana Bhat relishes the sight of his grandchildren playing all around the house and in the rice fields and the walnut orchards. He loves to run after them to stop them from plucking buds off the trees in the orchard. But he allows them to go amuck because his own childhood was bereft of such adventures and pranks. 'Mine was a no-childhood,' he laments. Zana Bhat is very hardworking. His dedication, honesty and uprightness set him apart from others because he avoids indulging in the money-lending business. 'It's not healthy, this money-lending business,' he confides to his family. 'We have all that we need.' Over the years, he has earned adequate wealth and respect that will last a lifetime. He takes pride in his achievements. It's evident by the way he conducts himself in the village.

IT'S a dark night. In the adjoining village, Watakul, there aren't any Pandit families. Yet a multitude has risen and come out in the streets. Zana Bhat and his family are clueless. They are in their warm beds, wondering what's causing the people of the village nearby to rise. Radhakrishan is not in his room. He's sleeping in the granary where grains and other household belongings are stocked. Zafar, the family help, is there too. Zafar is the one who looks after Radhakrishan as though he were his own child. He has taught Radhakrishan how to climb trees. Zafar's own children are in his village far away. It's a village of tribesmen. Zafar misses his children when he's with Radhakrishan. It is one such night when he can't bear the pangs of separation any more. He quietly looks at Radhakrishan's cherubic face and thanks his master, Zana Bhat, for giving him this job. Remembering the countless favours bestowed upon him by Zana Bhat and family, a tear trickles down his face.

A harsh knocking is heard. Moments later, Zana Bhat and nine members of his family are killed by intruders. But Zafar and Radhakrishan are missing. Within a span of thirty minutes everything changes. The floor and the walls of Zana Bhat's house turn red.

Zafar is running with Radhakrishan in his arms. They have left the house behind. Zafar is not able to fully fathom the enormity of the situation. He stops to catch his breath and rest. They look towards the house. It is in flames. A giant cloud of black smoke has spread across the sky.

ZAFAR reaches his village. He's exhausted. Radhakrishan is in his arms. He raises an alarm. He is frightened. He narrates the ordeal. He speaks of the horror. He reveals how four familiar peasants who once worked for Zana Bhat came to the house in the dead of the night and massacred the entire family. 'If you can't return the money to the family from whom you borrowed it, then kill the family,' says Zafar tearfully. 'That's what the cowardly peasants did. They killed my Master for his goodness. They killed the entire clan. Then they torched the house,' Zafar sobs. 'The peasants knocked on the door. When Baabi opened the door, the peasants pretended to be weary travellers and asked for water. Baabi recognised them. Everything ended when Baabi went into the kitchen to fetch water for them. The peasants spared no one,' Zafar cries.

The tribesmen accompanying Zafar gather and leave for Watakul, where they join the clueless men who believe that the Bhats died because the house caught fire. By the time the five hundred men reach the mound of ash—the Bhat Ashram—everything has perished. Only charred bones remain.

A police inquiry and several protests later, the four people found guilty are hanged at Lal Chowk. It isn't enough. It can never be. It leads to mass killings. The June of 1931 turns bloody.

YEARS pass. Radhakrishan is a young man now. He has dark hair. His eyebrows are thick and prominent. He's fair and tall and the handsomest man in the village. He's the apple of everyone's eyes. The village girls dote on him. They giggle whenever they see him working in the fields. They marvel at his looks.

It is the summer of 1947. The days demand toughness of the men and women. The summer has been bloody like the summer of 1931, Radhakrishan thinks. He sees these tall Kabaili tribesmen disguised as Pakistani rangers running around the village with swords in their hands. One day, he and Kamla, a young girl of twelve, escape narrowly from the jaws of death. Kabailis are everywhere, looking for people to kill. Radhakrishan is at once reminded of the night when he last kissed his mother goodnight. He hides behind the same tree that he climbed as a child. Zafar isn't around any more.

Radhakrishan and Kamla flee to Srinagar. They take shelter in the premises of a temple. Days pass. The creation of Pakistan has come at a cost. People continue to pay with their lives. Kashmir is a war zone. The Pandit households and shops are looted, women are raped in front of their kids, and those who retaliate are butchered. One day, Radhakrishan is having food. He smells blood everywhere. He wants to run away. He wants to escape the terror.

THE year is 1965. India is at war with Pakistan. The army is spread across Kanikoot. Pakistani army is creating havoc. Radhakrishan is abducted and tortured. He doesn't care much about himself but when he looks at the floor, at his own blood, he wants to go back to his beautiful wife, Kamla, and the three children back home. He wants to pick them up and run away from the wretched place.

Days later, one night, Radhakrishan sees some people beating a tall man mercilessly in the street. He manages to run away from the scene. He reaches home and seeks help for the man. Nothing is better, he thinks, than the warmth of home and the hugs of those tiny arms that call him Bobji.

IT is 1971. Radhakrishan is the village chowkidar now. He's fondly called Bobji by everyone. He is proud of being responsible for protecting the village at night. This is what gives him hope and strength. He protects the village from all potential attacks and vows to give a tough fight to any intruders who mean trouble. He's a changed man. He doesn't want to run. He wants to stay. This is his home, the land of his ancestors, and he hopes to die here.

IT'S the summer of 1986. Bobji's aging body is as tough as his spirit. He has four sons and three daughters who are scattered across the village and the city. His eldest son is married. Bobji is happy because he thinks his children are old enough to take care of themselves.

Then one day, the situation in Anantnag takes a deadly turn. Temples are demolished and desecrated. The idols of Gods and Goddesses inside the temples are stolen and smashed. Shops belonging to Pandits are vandalised. Houses are pelted with stones. Bobji's eldest daughter, Tosha, and Ramesh plead with Bobji to leave everything and flee to Delhi. 'Let us sell our land and go to Delhi, and start our life afresh,' they plead. But Bobji is adamant. This place is all they have. It is the only thing he has ever known. He wishes to live and die here, despite not knowing what's in store, much like the dreadful night of 1931.

IN the summer of 1991, the militants abducted Bobji. He was detained at a secret place for three days. A year earlier, the rest of his family had fled Kashmir after the political situation deteriorated. His eldest son had been abducted too. Earlier, in 1989, he had become a grandfather for the first time. At the time, he had advised the whole family to go to Jammu. But he had chosen to stay in Kashmir. Radhakrishan had a history of running away ever since he was a young boy of six.

In 2013, Bobji, who was now frail and in hospital, remembered that bright summer day of 1931 when his mother ran after him to prevent him from plucking apples and walnuts off the trees in their large orchard. He knew he was going to her. It would be his final run.

The keys to a house not there

Pratush Koul

AT the time when the results of the matriculation examination held by the University of Punjab, Lahore, in 1947 were announced, the partition of India and Pakistan had taken place, and students from the J&K who hadn't received their certificates were asked to collect the copies at Solan, Himachal Pradesh. After some years, my grandfather, Dwarika Nath Koul, was issued a certificate too. The year of issue written on the certificate is 1952. The delay had happened because of the cross-border migration of the members of staff and the teachers.

Just before the communal riots that took place in 1947, my grandfather had received a job offer that would have taken him to Muzzafarabad in Pakistan. Somehow, he didn't accept the offer. His refusal to migrate to Pakistan turned out to be a blessing in disguise. His maternal uncle, Jiya Lal Pandita, was a well-known priest at the Sharda Peeth temple, and was believed to have predicted the future events.

My grandfather had narrated an incident that had taken place in his childhood. He had tried planting a walnut sapling. Seeing his desperate attempt at planting the sapling, his uncle had said to him that although the tree would grow and bear fruit, it would be of no use to the family. Soon after, the riots forced my grandfather to leave his village. The family was never to see the tree and the walnuts. Grandfather's uncle wasn't able to return from Sharda Peeth, and after some time, he died.

This was not the only tragedy in the family. All through my childhood, my father kept narrating stories to me.

In 1947, when tribal militias from Pakistan raided Kashmir to occupy the territory, my father's grandfather, Niranjan Nath Raina (called *Taetha*) and his family were living in Pattan, near Baramulla. When the gun-wielding tribal militias reached the village, they ransacked the houses of Pandits for articles of monetary value. Then they looted the houses and butchered dozens of people in the locality. After looting and killing, they torched the houses. Niranjan Nath Raina's father survived the initial attacks. For days, he hid deep inside stacks of dry hay kept at the attic. But the tribal militia found him and burnt him alive. They then torched the entire house. They waited to see the house turn into a pile of rubble and ash. After witnessing this tragedy, my grandfather and family migrated from Pattan to Srinagar. They abandoned the 90 *kanals* of land they owned in Pattan. Several decades later, they lost most of it due to the Land Reforms Act of 1960.

One day, when my grandfather was rummaging through the contents of his old tin trunk, he stumbled upon a book written in Urdu. It was titled *Umeed Ki Rah*. The book contained sayings of Jesus Christ. Christian missionaries active in Kashmir in the 70s distributed such books to the Hindus to convert them to

Christianity. The book was one of the few things that grandfather preserved.

My father was born in Ali Kadal, Srinagar, in 1958. At the time, grandfather was working as a Post Master in Srinagar. The family was living on rent. Grandfather and father decided to build a house of their own. In 1974, they started building a new house in Habba Kadal. The construction lasted nine years. After the house was built, the family stayed in it for seven years.

The violence of the late 80s didn't impact them much, as they had witnessed similar incidents of violence all through their lives. They nurtured hope. But, years later, in the autumn of 1989, the killing of Tika Lal Taploo, the prominent leader, brought back the fear of persecution. Then there were other signs. My mother was working in the social welfare department and was posted in Baramulla. One particular day, sensing the outbreak of violence in the vicinity, her colleagues asked her to leave the workplace early. She travelled from Baramulla to Srinagar in a bus teeming with protesters who chanted slogans of *Azadi* (Kashmir's freedom from India). She hid her gold earrings and removed her *bindi* (the earrings and the bindi were signs of her religious identity). Fear persisted in her heart.

In January 1990, my grandparents and my mother's family migrated to Jammu. My father (unmarried at the time) migrated to Jammu too.

In 2014, my father and I undertook a trip to Kashmir. He took me to Habba Kadal in Srinagar to see our house there. I was fifteen years old at the time. I was excited at the prospect of seeing the house my father and grandfather had built. When we reached Habba Kadal, the house wasn't there. Father was heartbroken. We got to know that after the exodus of my father and grandfather, the house had been torched.

Recently, while getting the walls of our house in Jammu painted, my parents chanced upon a bunch of keys hidden inside an old box kept on a shelf. Father held the keys close to his chest. Mother broke down. I asked them about the keys. They made me sit next to them and told me about each one of the keys. 'This big key unlocked the drawing room,' they said. 'This small one unlocked the kitchen. This one unlocked the bedroom, and this one unlocked the granary,' they went on and on.

Dad and mom then handed over the keys to me. I wondered if the keys served a purpose any more. Of what value were they now?

I realised that the bunch of keys to a house not there might be the most valuable possession of our family.

In the summer of 2007 when I was in Class 4, I saw thousands of tents in the open fields at Mishriwala, Jammu. My mother had taken me along to visit her friend who lived nearby. At first, I thought the tents belonged to nomads and shepherds. I saw people queuing up to fill water at a hand pump. I saw children like me drenched in sweat and loitering around without any purpose. Nothing made sense to me at the time. Little did I know that the people occupying the tents were from my community. Some of our family friends lived there too. These people were homeless. Once they too had houses. Now, all they were left with were keys to houses that were not there.

The village of vacant houses

Seema Bhat

A few years ago, in the autumn of 2008, I undertook a trip to Kashmir. It had been close to two decades since I had visited my roots there. While driving from Srinagar to Haal, I became very anxious and emotional. Haal had been the village of my childhood. To embrace the memories of my childhood for the first time in two decades wasn't easy. Even though we had lived in Srinagar for some years before leaving Kashmir in 1990, my heart was always closer to Haal. I would always wait for the vacations to go back to the place.

All those years, I never realised that Haal would turn out to symbolise a way of life that had flourished in Kashmir for centuries. While we were cruising along the Srinagar-Pulwama road, I imagined the walnut trees, the stream which flowed next to our house, the water mill, children playing in the courtyard of houses, the big *Kanj* in the middle of the village, the temple bells. The memory of the fabulous times came alive. I had been disconnected for the last two decades. Would everything be the same now? I wondered.

Finally I reached Haal. I ran towards my house, but to my utter dismay, I could see nothing except a dilapidated structure. The house was in ruins and I wept profusely at the sight of other dilapidated houses nearby. The water in the stream had dried up, and the water mill was gone. There were no children in the courtyard and the temple was caged behind barbed wire because the paramilitary forces were guarding it. I recollected my childhood days. How I would wake up in the morning, go to the temple holding the hand of my grandmother, and along the way the neighbours would greet us. I would meet the potter and ask him to make some earthen utensils for me so I could play with them. He would be delighted to oblige me. I would explore the village. The stream, the water mill, the walnut trees, the rice fields were my haunts. Everything was so pristine.

Haal may have seemed like any other village in Kashmir, but it was a village which represented the culture of Kashmiri Pandits in several ways. Those days, it symbolised a way of life that had remained untainted for centuries. It was unique in its landscape, geography and demography. The inhabitants were proud of the village. People there were highly educated and though many had left to seek jobs in Srinagar they hadn't abandoned their bonds with the village.

Even now, after twenty-eight years of living in exile, the Pandits who once lived in Haal refuse to sell their houses there. The structures are broken but they hold the last breath of a civilization that is centuries old.

Most of the landscape there has changed over the years but the beauty has remained unblemished. I wonder if the original inhabitants of this village still nurture hope to go back and rebuild their homes.

The place had something pure and chaste—ladies gossiping at *Yarbal* (embankment) in the evening, elders sitting in the shade of the massive chinar trees next to the Ganesh temple. The whole village would celebrate birthdays of people and participate wholeheartedly in festive occasions. We were one big family.

There would be many such villages in Kashmir that boast of a similar composite culture but none of them are thriving now. The villages bear no trace of the Pandits. The history of Pandits has been completely erased from them.

Yet Haal is different. The desolate and decrepit houses bear testament to the Pandit heritage. What remains now is just a faint shadowy trace that is on the verge of extinction. This faint trace will haunt the future generations of Kashmir.

I took several photographs of the empty houses, knowing that the houses might not last long. The broken and vacant houses speak of an era that was glorious and happy. I still remember the day when my mother and father left our ancestral house in Haal to go to Srinagar. They left because they wanted my brother and me to study in a school in Srinagar. They left everything because of us. It was a big sacrifice they made. That day was the saddest day of my life.

I dream of going back and reviving old bonds. I dream of rebuilding my ancestral house and planting a sapling in the garden there! I long for the beautiful past to return.

The home I dream of returning to

Nipa Charagi

IN the winter of 1990, when Kashmir decided it had no room for Pandits, and Jammu was creating space for them, our rented house in Delhi was also in a state of flux. My mother and I were in Delhi with my father, who at the time was the editor of the Urdu newspaper *Quami Awaz*. Who would have imagined that our holiday would turn into an extended stay?

Our two-room flat was always full of people looking to stay for a few days, unsure of what to do next. I remember one particular day. There must have been around a dozen people in the house, and just when it seemed we could accommodate no more people, the doorbell rang around midnight. There was yet another person fleeing from home. He stood at the door, holding a small bag. My mother, not sure what to do, asked the visitor to make himself comfortable.

That's how it was for most Kashmiri Pandit families in the valley as militancy gained ground and chants of *aazadi* (freedom) rented the air. They were forced to leave their homes and seek shelter in camps, rented houses, at relatives' places—sometimes in the tiniest of places, sometimes in the largest of hearts.

The struggle, the pain, the loss, and the consequences have manifested in many ways, and every time they echo in some form, you grieve for what has been lost.

MY grandmother, Radhamali, or Kakeni as she was fondly called, died in Srinagar in 1984, much before militancy started. Sometimes I feel she was lucky not to have gone through the misery of being uprooted from the only home she knew.

Kakeni ventured out of the state only once when my aunt took her to Haridwar. It was a momentous occasion. Everybody wanted her to wear a sari. She used to dress in the traditional attire of *pheran* (long tunic tied at the waist with a sash) and *taranga*, an elaborate headgear with several components and minute details. The *pheran* was not just a garment. It was a warm, embracing world. In winters, my sister and I would sit with our feet tucked inside the folds of her *pheran* while she held the *kangri* (firepot). The deep pockets of the garment always held some candy or coins for us.

Kakeni's favourite spot was next to the window in the room adjoining the kitchen on the ground floor, the big radio behind her; she would tune in every morning right after offering prayers facing the sun. From this vantage point, she could see who was coming in or going out of the house. The one thing she loved was watching the American sitcom *I Love Lucy.* She would be in giggles, though she did not understand English.

There is one particular image of Kakeni that has stayed with me. She is standing at the window of the first-floor room, looking out, with her hands resting on the ledge. Another memory is of the symbol 'Aum' tattooed on her hand. I would often rub it, thinking it would come off.

Kakeni's *pherans* were kept neatly folded in a trunk in a room on the top floor (called *kaeni*)—of no significance to those who would ransack the house years later. In summers we would sleep in this room, a poster of Shiva and Parvati looking down at us from an alcove. On one of the shelves were kept brass vessels, scrubbed and sparkling, ready to be lent to relatives and neighbours for use during wedding ceremonies.

When Kakeni came back from Haridwar, she got us two steel tumblers with our names etched in Hindi on the base. Surprisingly, one of the tumblers has travelled with us through the years, the etching still faintly visible.

My grandfather died when my father was still in college; the family falling on hard times. This is what shaped my father in a way. Money and he were not good companions though I doubt he ever missed its absence. He was man driven by his emotions. He began his career as a journalist for an English newspaper but later joined *Quami Awaz*. Even during the peak of militancy in Kashmir he was bringing out an edition of the newspaper from Srinagar. Eventually, it had to be shut, as the situation got worse.

My father died in Kolkata, far away from the house on Nai Sarak in Srinagar which my grandfather, Dina Nath, or Lala as he was called, had bought in the 1940s. We have a photograph of my dad and mom standing in the main doorway of the house, my mom pregnant with her first child. My sister Bablu and I were born there; I had always imagined retuning to this house no matter how far I drifted from it. It was not a physical structure, it was the sum total of us all: a repository of memories, of good times and bad, of people and relations, of the passage of time and seasons. It is what kept us rooted.

We shared the house with the Mattoos, to whom half the

portion was sold after Lala's death. The house was literally split down the middle—two mirror images, with a common staircase, entrance and landing areas. There was Tatha, the head of the family, his wife Bhabi, and their children, Dura, Kaka, Raja. Nana and Sabha—people who have loved us unconditionally. My sister and I were part of every celebration of theirs. We tagged along everywhere. Nana and Raja would feed us off their plates, and we can be seen gawking in their wedding album.

Kaka and Kakeni shared a special bond. My father had a habit of smoking only half a cigarette and then stubbing it out. My grandmother liked to take a few puffs once or twice a day, not openly though. As for Kaka, he rarely had the money to buy cigarettes. So both would steal dad's half-smoked cigarettes from the ashtray. When there were no half cigarettes, they would buy and share a cigarette, she taking a couple of deep puffs, he smoking the rest of it. Sabha was once caught smoking by my dad and given a good dressing down. He continues to be a non-smoker.

The Mattoos used to call my dad *Saebtoth* (a person who you love deeply). When Kaka's children, Rinku and Renu, were born, my mother became their *baddi* (elder) mummy. Now when we come together at weddings and deaths, we hug each other tightly, trying to hold on to the old times for a little bit longer.

This world of two unrelated families, brought together by a house, disintegrated in the face of militancy. The Mattoo siblings are settled in different cities. We connect on phone, sometimes on Facebook. Elsewhere in Kashmir, the same story was playing out. Extended and joint families that had lived together for generations ceased to exist as one unit. A way of life was lost forever.

WE spent a greater part of the nearly three-month winter vacation in Jammu, where my father would rent a flat near Residency Road. As we would leave the hills, the landscape would change, and with it, our friends and neighbours.

The two-storeyed building in Jammu had two floors with four flats. On the ground floor lived two Dogra families, the Sharmas and the Handas. On the first floor, facing our flat lived the Bhats, who, like us, would visit Jammu only in winter. Like the house in Srinagar, this one too had a common staircase running through the middle. And instead of a *kaeni* (attic), there was a huge common terrace. Here, warm, sunny afternoons would be spent chatting, shelling peanuts, flying kites, and hanging out on cots.

Mr Bhat and Ameena had two sons, Biju and Bublaa. The boys called their mother Mamai, and dad, Bhaiji. So did we. My sister was the eldest in our group of four, and I the youngest. The evenings would be spent in our flat—the two moms, four school-going children, and our grandmother. There was no TV, radio or phone. Only the Handas had a TV on which we would sometimes watch *Chitrahaar*. Our friends were the Sharmas' children with whom we would converse in Dogri. On Sundays, their flat would smell of *rajma-chawal* and *desi ghee*.

The Bhats used to live a few kilometres away from our house in Srinagar, but our paths would rarely cross there. In Jammu, whenever Mamai took me to the market with her, people would mistake me for her daughter.

Biju was a Feroze Khan fan; Bublaa was crazy about Mithun Chakraborty. They had pasted huge posters of these Bollywood stars on the walls of their room; they knew every dialogue of their films by heart. Their pocket money was spent on buying tickets to watch movies. When they had no money, they would peek through the doors of Uttam Cinema hall to catch snatches of the movie playing inside. They were like film critics, deciding which movies were suitable for us to watch.

We would learn later that Mamai was also greatly enamoured of Bollywood movies. One day she came home with a photograph in which she was posing like Saira Banu. Dressed in trousers, shirt, with a purple bandana tied around her head, she was standing with one leg placed on a chair, one hand resting on a high table. Mr Bhat, a man of few words, was furious. It is not known what became of the picture.

By the end of February, our holdalls and suitcases would be packed, ready to head back to Srinagar.

This world also disintegrated when we left Srinagar. We have lost touch with the Bhats. I have no idea what turn their lives have taken. But I often wonder how their world must have changed when militants forced cinema halls in the Kashmir valley to shut down.

MY mother visited the house in Srinagar, no longer ours, in the early 2000s. She took Gulla the milkman with her. She went to her room and saw the owners' two daughters studying near the window, much like my sister and I did. On the top floor, a carved pillar was missing, maybe plundered when the house was unoccupied. When the lady of the house asked my mom if she was the previous owner, my mother says she burst into tears.

Gulla and Siddha, brothers, were the milkmen in our neighbourhood. Their cowshed was the place to fetch milk and also catch up on neighbourhood news. If somebody wanted to enquire about a girl or a boy for a marriage proposal, they came here. Their clientele largely comprised Pandits. If my grandmother ever visited their home next to the sprawling cowshed, they would offer her a bowl of fresh cream as a token of their respect.

I remember I was in school when my mother was admitted to a hospital for surgery. It was Gulla who was entrusted with the task of taking my sister and me to visit her there. He was the man who came looking for me when curfew was imposed suddenly one day. There are people you have faith in—faith that remains unshaken with time and distance.

Most of the houses in our neighbourhood belonged to

Pandits, while the shops were run by Muslims. There was Maqbool's grocery shop; the tailor's shop where our *pherans* were stitched; the men's barber shop; Rasheed the butcher's shop; Manna, the cobbler; Kanderni, the bread seller, and her son Bashir, who would call my dad Mohanji; and Rashid, the wood craftsman.

Then there was Amma-*guer*, who sold milk, *paneer* (cottage cheese) and curd. Men in the locality would gather in his shop in the mornings and evenings, to read the newspaper and discuss politics. He had two daughters and a son. The son moved to Bengaluru to study. He visited us in Delhi once with a box of pastries; he had got a job in the US. Amma-*guer*, the boisterous man with a booming voice, died some years ago. I wonder if there is a dairy shop on that street now where people hang out.

Our house shared a wall and fence with the Saprus, three brothers who lived in one house. They shared a wall and fence with the Kouls, who had a dog named Sheebu. Adjoining our house on the other side was a Muslim family, which kept aloof. Opposite this row of four houses was the sprawling house of Daddy and Rajlal, and their three daughters. Their house and lawn were always used for weddings in the neighbourhood. Their granddaughter was my schoolmate. I remember us walking to the school bus stop with Jumma (their servant) accompanying us sometimes. Most days it was Kakeni who would see us off.

Nai Sarak ran parallel to Ganpathiyar (famous for its Ganesh temple) and led up to Habba Kadal, also a Pandit-dominated locality. While the distance from Nai Sarak to Habba Kadal was short, you could easily spend one to two hours going and coming because of the number of people you would meet and talk to on the way. Sometimes, you would even forget the reason for stepping out of the house. Straight down Habba Kadal, we would reach my aunt's house on the riverfront in Bana mohalla. If we turned left and crossed the Habba Kadal Bridge, we would reach my eldest aunt's house in Bal Garden, with its two fountains in the front lawn.

These vibrant streets, always abuzz with life, fell silent in 1990; the houses became deserted and forlorn. They must have finally made way for new families and started breathing again with a fresh coat of paint over old memories. Maybe the families in our row bond with each other, like we used to do, over the fence, exchanging gossip and bowls of curries unless they have built walls that cannot be scaled.

I left home without saying goodbye. If I had known what was to unfold, I would have packed with a little more thought, carried bits of my childhood, my teenage years—the diary in which I would jot down my rambling thoughts, the framed photograph of dad hanging on the wall, mom's pink Banarasi sari and the maroon brocade pouch with a drawstring, the inland letters, read, re-read and kept neatly folded in the cupboard.

There was a kind of impermanence in our lives in those initial years in Delhi. The city intimidated me. I had lost contact with friends in Srinagar, had no information on how they were dealing with the turmoil. We lived in intense fear; my father was receiving death threats. And most news coming from home was not good.

On February 13, 1990, around 7:15 in the evening, a close friend of my father was shot dead outside his house in Srinagar, his old parents oblivious to the tragedy unfolding outside the gates of their house. He was Lassa Kaul, the director of Doordarshan Kendra. *Lassa* means 'the blessed one'. You can see how sadness envelops his daughter even after all these years. She was a teenager then. She says she has outgrown other tragedies in her life, but the death of her father continues to haunt her. Not a day passes when she does not think of him. She and her brother used to call him Kaka, and he would playfully tell her: *Hatai kodmai vanth*. (There is no English translation of this term of endearment).

She calls herself an eternal refugee with no sense of

belonging. She misses her home, but the longing is soaked with pain, sometimes anger. Her father, despite threats to his life, had faith that he would not be harmed. After all this was his home. He belonged here. But those seeking "freedom" had no place for him.

The Kauls had moved into this new house in Bemina in October 1989. They had been there only three months when the tragedy struck. The house was sold; the family couldn't bear to keep it. His daughter says sometimes she wishes they had retained the house, for, in a way, it tied them to that place.

Sometimes you don't want to let go of the pain, afraid that you will be left with nothing to hold on to. Every Kashmiri who left has a story, just like every Kashmiri who stayed back has one.

One of my uncles, his three sons and their families took refuge in a migrant camp in Delhi. They used to live in a large house on the riverbank in Srinagar. In the camp, they shared a large hall with other families, a bedcover draped over a rope providing some semblance of privacy. Soon after arriving in Delhi, my uncle strolled out of the camp one day. If he lost his way that morning, he never found it back. His dead body was discovered after several days. His children live in different places, united in their loss and grief.

Delhi introduced me to a world that was not hemmed in by mountains—the horizon was broader. If Srinagar was like a gentle river, calm and unhurried, Delhi was a giant cement mixer—noisy, harsh, always in a churn. Our first real home was the two-room flat not very far from the railway station, the first stop for relatives and friends arriving in the city. It had an amazing capacity to accommodate everyone. In the multi-storeyed buildings of this society, simply identified by alphabets from A to F, there were people who walked into our lives and made us their friends. They introduced us to the city, making it less intimidating, and easier to navigate.

When I pass those buildings, I am filled with a warm feeling. This was also home-like. I often wonder how I would react if I were to visit our house in Srinagar. I know it would not be easy. Its rhythms must have changed. It used to be spruced up in the run-up to Shivratri, every corner dusted and aired, the crisp winter air filling the house. Now it must dress up for Eid. Every street-facing window of the house would be occupied during the Janmashtami procession; my mother would be downstairs frying fritters, the aroma wafting up. Nobody would now be leaving a plate of *gaad-batta* (fish and rice) in the attic for the deity of the house—the plate covered with a wicker basket, a glass of water and a burning lamp left on the side. As for the crow's perch in the garden, I wonder if anybody remembers to put a handful of rice on it before sitting down for lunch.

Perhaps a tourist would not find anything amiss on that street; the homes and people would look warm and inviting; the shops, bustling. She would, however, not know of the grandfather who would take a cold-water bath at the crack of dawn and walk to Durganag every single day; the uncle who would walk barefoot to Hari Parbat; the mother who would head to Tulla Mulla on *Zaeth Aetham* and return home with *lucchi-halva* (flat bread and pudding); the grandmother who would drink tea from a *khos* (brass cup). The tourist would not know that if she were to peel away the paint on the walls around the main doors of those three houses in a row, it would reveal vines of flowers and leaves, painted during weddings and Yagnopavit ceremonies, with an Aum symbol drawn on the top. It would be difficult for her to imagine the circumstances in which the Pandit families in this neighbourhood and other parts of Kashmir abandoned their homes.

She would not know because the people who could tell her about life in those neighbourhoods before militancy do not live there anymore.

When you are separated from "home", it turns up in unexpected places. In my Kolkata home, its smell is wrapped up in an old cotton cloth containing two Kashmiri shawls purchased by my late in-laws when they visited Srinagar as tourists in 1981. My mother-in-law's jewellery is kept in a small, intricately carved wooden box bought on that holiday. The taste and flavour of home is stashed away in a plastic bag in the fridge containing dried vegetables; in the side compartment is a tiny, transparent box of saffron.

"Home" turns up at a memorial service when Dhananjay Kaul sings Lal Ded's *vakh*: '*Zuv chum bramaan, gara gatshaha*' *(My heart yearns for home*). As people pay tributes, the reference to home and large extended families comes up often. You glance around the room and see familiar faces, some of whom have grown old beyond their years, dabbing their eyes. Then your aunt consoles you by saying, '*Kormai chashmaen myueth*' (A kiss on your eyes). And in that moment you realise that people like her, who speak in the language of the past, are dwindling.

My father would herald winters in Delhi by embracing his *pheran*. He felt at home. Then he would say, '*Kangir josh ghais hai asun*' (*What's missing is a firepot*). His memory would take him back to the 'warmest place on earth', which turned unusually cold one winter twenty-eight years ago.

Lost window

Neeraj Santoshi

I remember looking at the rain one afternoon through the window of my ancestral house in Kashmir. My grandfather, Tathya, was telling me a story about a King who had lost his kingdom. I had irked him by asking continuously why the King had lost his kingdom and why he had to leave his land. Tathya loved to tell stories and I loved to listen. I loved the way he would punctuate them with his inimitable 'May Mother Goddess protect you!'

The trail of the long forgotten scenes is set in exile. The ancient seeds are lost in the belly of the earth.

It is raining here today. Some ancient water wells up in my searching eyes. I know windows are absences; absences in the walls. But sometimes windows can themselves get walled in one's memory as fixtures. When it rains in my village, that window where Tathya told me numerous stories misses me too. Its frame is a picture pregnant with a thousand questions. He who has an eye can see the 'familiar absence'.

Windows have always appeared to me very mysterious. But the window of my grandfather's stories was my first window to the world, literally and metaphorically. It was at that window I had for the first time seen the wonders of rain and seasons and the few pretty neighbourhood girls, whom, I later realised, I could not have loved. No regrets. Am I speaking the truth? Zorba must be laughing somewhere.

Whenever there is a downpour I miss that window here so far away from home. Rain was my companion for years. Those were the days when I would let raindrops touch my eyes. I have lost my little window to rain, to my past, to my own small world. I don't know how that window feels when nobody looks at the new blossoms and the bulbuls and the rain through it.

It is raining and the night is immensely beautiful. Whenever it rains here, tears of gratitude for that window also fall from my eyes. The absence of that window has somehow added perspective to my life.

Whatever I see, I feel I am seeing through it. Or I imagine so. I want this world to be seen through that window.

The sound of rain in the windy winter night is so attractive. Cold shivers go down my spine and some ancient longing is awakened. In the rain, I feel someone in the distance calling, someone beyond age, and someone beyond mountains and clouds. I feel the ancient movement and struggles. I feel the beat of ages in the patter of rain. I feel the mystic wriggle.

The memories of my childhood touch the inner strings. Does rain remind us of the comfort of mother's womb where everything one needed was given to us without asking?

I can still see it clearly like it was yesterday: The childhood image of looking at the sky through the window. It never leaves me. I used to wonder where all these drops came from and how high in the sky I could see a single drop and follow its fall and its final kiss on earth. I used to watch the play of drops for hours. It was then that I understood the power of a single drop, and how far the ripples go and the fact that they never actually stop.

When it rains a strange unrest clouds my inner sky. There are flashes. In the darkness I see something in the distance so beautiful. I want to go out far away to where I can dance in the rain, leaving all my clothes far behind. Rain and me! Wish Zorba could jump out and dance with me and become rain.

To a worldly person all this might seem romantic. Maybe, that is true. In this shrinking world, romanticism masks the imperfections and gives you a feel of the translucent beauty amidst the harsh realities.

Somewhere, an all-pervading voyeuristic eye is noticing all our moves. How to see a dream? How to make love? How to say 'no' to 'How to…' My window! And the rain!

Don't I need to leave behind my raincoat? Has the window of the computer screen become my window to the world? Does a deliberate romanticism or a self-chosen illusion help me make the harsh edges palpable? Is the mouse taking me down the hole?

Somewhere in the distance a familiar song is in the air. I love the snow ambience of the song. It reminds me of the snowy mountains near which we lived. Will I get distanced from my roots slowly inch by inch? Will folds obliterate my view?

This reminds me of what Tathya told me once near the window, when I was low after having lost a cricket match to a rival team whose captain eyed my neighbourhood girl: 'Nothing stops in the eternal flux. The raindrops the girl next door receives in her palm must have been a cloud. Learn to see things differently and you will never feel low again. See a thing or a face as if you are seeing it for the first time. See a thing or a face as if you are looking at it for the last time.'

Music, memories and rain have a common link. Rain is music. The first drop on the parched lips of earth was primal music, primal sound—the mother of all sounds. It set the symphony going.

Rain saturates my being. Night is immensely dark and the wind makes the leaves rustle and stirs primal desires in me. Here it stops. Here it starts again slowly. Each leaf dances its own unique dance.

Rain becomes more severe. Its patter on the roof is more audible now. If death comes, it should come in a moment without any sound. Like a feather falling slowly from a bird's nest! Like a long forgotten friend suddenly opening the door and embracing you. Like a song you have heard in childhood. Like a drop of water kissing a seed sleeping in the lap of earth! And the seed sacrificing itself for a future seed, a branch, a flower, and dreaming of romancing the elusive moon!

Isn't rain earth's answer to eternal quest, eternal invitation for the penetration of its deeper mysteries? Isn't every raindrop a love letter of the distant clouds to beloved earth, of desires hidden to the fragrances adrift, of the oceans to the mighty mountains? And doesn't the earth take every letter to its heart and answer in blossoms, in the freshness of the green grass, in the sweetness of the fruits, in the blue of the gushing mountain-spring.

I wish before my frame returns to the elements or the frame of that window returns to the elements, we meet and watch the seasons change again as I used to years ago sitting next to my grandfather.

Tathya's stories will never end, though his own story ended on his eightieth birthday, half a decade after his exodus from home. He looked at Pir Panjal and faded away. Tathya still tells stories through me, but in the absence of that window, the stories miss something. Familiar absence!

Tathya, I still do not understand why the King lost his kingdom…

Literature in exile

Agnishekhar

EXILE is a very frightful and agonising condition that begs many questions. The world has been changing for the past so many years. The changes are puzzling and astonishing. Globalisation, information technology and politics have brought about tremendous changes in the sensibility of man. We find possibilities and uncertainties, development and fear, progress and despair. Instability, terror, displacement and migrations are realities of life. Economic compulsions, ambitions of the corporate world and the transfer of lands have given rise to migrations. Migration is not a new phenomenon. The world saw this during the two world wars. Even the natural calamities made this happen. The partition of India in 1947 witnessed a migration of great magnitude. We witnessed it in the case of refugees from Tibet, Bangladesh,

Pakistan and Afghanistan.

The migration of around five hundred thousand Kashmiri Pandits from Kashmir in 1990 is the most tragic migration of modern India. It happened due to religious intolerance, jihad and terrorism. Terrorism and jihad, aided and abetted by Pakistan, uprooted an indigenous and old civilization. This uprootedness was the result of gruesome killings, inhuman treatment of a community, violence, oppression, tyranny, maiming of limbs, kidnappings, threats, rape, arson and burning of houses. This tragedy exposed the incompetence, hollowness and pettiness of the Indian State.

This migration gave rise to a number of questions about the fate and future of Indian secularism and democracy. The jihadis either reject secularism, democracy, coexistence and religious tolerance as unIslamic or impose conditions upon others for living on their terms. The politics behind all this breaks the myth of conventional Indian polity. We have to look at all these things from a different point of view and find new definitions and meanings of secularism.

We have to find out the reasons behind the forced exile of half a million Kashmiri Pandits. What was the objective and motive behind all this? Could these Pandits stop the Muslims of Kashmir who formed the majority from creating a theocratic, Islamic republic, or from opting for the merger with Pakistan? Were the Pandits militarily, politically and economically so strong and powerful? The answer is a big 'No'. Kashmiri Pandits represented our five-thousand-year-old civilizational continuity. Muslims, religious zealots and terrorists could not come to terms with this fact. Our civilizational continuity was a link with the ancient Indian culture, its ethos, aesthetics, philosophy and religion.

The noted Indologist, Kapila Vatsyayan, saw Kashmir as the 'crucible of Indian civilization'. In her view, 'the exodus of Kashmiri Pandits is the exodus of that crucible'. For ages Kashmir has been known for free and frank debates and discourses on intellectual and philosophical matters. Kashmir stood for the intermingling of Naga cult, Shaivism, Buddhism, Vaishnavism and other trends. The currents and cross-currents of various philosophies met, broke, synthesised and took new shapes in Kashmir. Kashmir is the fountainhead of Indian poetics and history. Callous indifference towards the exodus of Pandits from Kashmir shows the injustice and criminality against the soul, character and ethos of India. This tragic migration of a chunk of Kashmiri society did not become a point of discussion and debate for the academicians, intellectuals and opinion makers in India. For the so-called secular and progressive forces, the mass migration of Pandits was not disturbing at all. They concealed it from the Indian public and ignored this burning problem. All this was done under a plan and conspiracy hatched by these forces. They did not even mention the far-reaching consequences of this catastrophe.

Under these conditions, it was only the Kashmiri Pandit poets, short story writers and artists who rose to the occasion and produced literature that reflects the agony and pain of the exiled community. Consciousness of history made them express their horrible conditions with a view to find their roots. These writers shouted their pain, anger and shame through their writings in Kashmiri, Hindi, Urdu, Punjabi and English. They gave vent to their rage, hurt, restlessness and uprootedness to paint painful pictures of their yearning for their homeland. Their writings reflect their experiences of the impact of terrorism and militancy on their psyche. Khema Kaul in her poem *The Return* laments:

You are
in blood
in agony,
and
we are
lost.

This literature shows the resistance of the Pandits to the destructive forces. The agonising experience gave rise to the literature of resistance and protest. In spite of the provocations, the exiled writers stood firm and protected their age-long traditional value system. While fighting religious extremism, violence and communalism of the Muslims, the writers clung to the human values. They paid attention to the new face of terrorism and its tentacles. They projected the torture of displacement and migration. They celebrated memory, wrote about nostalgia, legends, history and dreams. A K Rehbar in his short story *Roots* writes:

> Had I secured a job here I would not find myself in this sorry state now. I had made doleful entreaties to each and every officer but it was no use... All our property was taken over without compensation in the guise of reforms and we were, so to say, clean-shaven. Reforms as such are acceptable to me too but the way they gobbled up our lands is simply atrocious. The other day I went to my daughter's house. You should have seen how her husband and three brothers-in-law, along with their families, are huddled together in rooms not bigger than pigeon holes. The poor fellows once possessed twenty to thirty *kanals* of land but they were not wise enough to set apart a piece of land on which they could build a large house later.

The Kashmiri Pandit writers created a new genre of writing—exile literature. A significant dimension of exile is found in 'premonition' described in the literature. The six migrations in the history of Kashmiri Pandits speak of religious persecution, deaths, destruction, forced conversions and torture. These are in the memory of the community. The literature written at present abounds in 'premonition' for the readers find protest there. There is no desire for revenge. Harikrishna Kaul in his short story *Hangul* describes this in a veiled manner:

> He left around 10 in the morning on a Sunday to see Anand Bhawan where Jawaharlal was born and Indira brought up. While leaving, he thought: 'Will I be able to catch a bus? A rickshaw will charge too much.'
>
> He came back and entered his house. Nana was kissing his wife's neck, breasts and lips. He had got a gold chain and was about to put it around her neck when father opened the door. Nana's wife gave a shriek. Nana couldn't control himself. He shot a word at his father. Father was embarrassed and turned around. He left the house and spent the time on the road.
>
> Nana's arrow-like word followed him.
>
> 'Do you hear?'
>
> He got up from sleep. He had heard Nana shouting. He did not know what he had said. He went on looking at him like a hangul.... dumbfounded.

The Kashmiri Pandit is referred to as hangul—a stag on the brink of extinction.

Terrorism and migration are the themes in modern Indian literature particularly poetry. Kashmiri Pandit poets and writers were not hounded out of Kashmir because they were writers and scholars. Nor did the Pandit writers opt for exile. They were forced to leave Kashmir because they were Hindus. In exile they feel helpless and uprooted and struggle for survival amidst the torture and pain of life. They depict the complexities and horrifying aspects of 'exiled' life. They write about personal, family and community lives. They talk about identity crisis, diaspora, ethnic cleansing, pain and terrifying memories. Rattan Jowhar in his poem *Each Moment* writes:

> Who will listen?
> Blood stained swords
> run incessantly across the veins
> and hearts are agitated.

Makhan Lal Kanwal in the poem *The Song of Light* expresses his anger thus:

The whole sank in darkness.
Benumbed and wonderstruck,
darkness swallowed
the breaths of light.
Urns are silent.

Restlessness, desire for freedom, hope, doubt, suspicion, apprehension and protest are the other dominant themes of our literature. The Hindi poetry of Khema Koul, Maharaj Krishan Santoshi, Rattan Lal Shant, M K Bharat and Shashi Shekhar Toshkhani is nearer to the literature produced by the Jews and the Black Africans. The Kashmiri Pandit writers and their writings connect us with the Tibetans and the Palestinians. The desire of the exiles for their homeland Kashmir reminds the readers of the refrain: *See you in Jerusalem.*

In exile, the social life of Kashmiri Pandits is destabilised. Theirs is a sordid existence. They are discriminated against. This discrimination is a new kind of apartheid. Som Nath Zutshi in his short story *Who are these Daryodanas?* expresses his condition as:

> Suddenly a proclamation rang out, 'Caution! Be warned! On your guard!' Stout staffs hit the gates of houses as the calls came. At this, life returned to the cowering humans—at least someone was alive! And the loud outcry rose to a crescendo. Countless hordes gathered in the field; some with broken visages, some half-dead. Out of the multitude came a powerful voice, 'Do not panic, countrymen! It is not night. This black pall will soon vanish and there will be light once again!'
> Another cry rose to counter this claim, 'The sun is gone. How long can living things survive?' The first voice retorted, 'Did not the skies darken at mid-day during the war of the Mahabharata? I tell you there is no cause for panic.' 'But that was only a momentary night brought about by Lord Krishna in order to destroy falsehood, whereas this night has lasted for days and months now. Where will we find a Krishna to fold up this darkness? This night is much more cruel than the night in the Mahabharata.'

Moti Lal Saqi, the noted Kashmiri poet, critic and researcher, said that exiles are the 'new untouchables of democracy'. I feel that Kashmiri Pandits in exile are the new untouchables of Indian secularism. This kind of protest is seen in the Kashmiri poetry of Arjan Dev Majboor, Tej Rawal, Rattan Jowhar and others. They shout their pain and anger against all that happened.

Two chairpersons of India's Human Rights Commission have expressed their unhappiness over the condition of the exiles. Their statements show bitterness for the situation that the exiles live in. Justice Ranganath Mishra, the former Chairman of the National Human Rights Commission (NHRC), said that the plight of Kashmiri Pandits is akin to genocide. Former Justice Dr Adarsh Sen Anand called the life of Kashmiri Pandit exiles 'animal existence'.

We, Kashmiri Pandit exiles, are scattered throughout India. That is why in our struggle there is no intensity and force which is present in the struggle of those who live in their homeland amidst political turmoil. That makes our struggle all the more challenging. This predicament is reflected in the poetry of these poets who write in Kashmiri, Urdu and English. The poets no doubt write about heart-rending situations, circumstances and trials and tribulations of day-to-day life. They write about the pain of existence, insomnia, psychological diseases, problems faced by the children and the effect of migration on the education of children. The imagery is highly disturbing. Maharaj Krishen Santoshi in his poem *Sign* reflects:

I live
in the midst of signs
where
my name
is
a sign
a number
and
not a word.

The plots of his short stories are centred on the homeland. These make the literature in exile home-centric.

Questions arise: Should we compare the plight of the Kashmiri Pandits with the condition of the Jews in the concentration camps and the gas chambers? During World War II, the Jews had to undergo unimaginable torture and torment. Attempts were made to exterminate all Jews, their culture and traditions. The poems, stories, novels, letters, diaries, films and other writings shock and stun us even today. Have the Kashmiri Pandit exiles had such horrifying experiences? Did anybody make gas chambers and concentration camps for us?

The difference between history and literature is that history records dates and details of the happenings, whereas literature presents sensibilities of man. Certainly there were no separate gas chambers for the Kashmiri Pandits in Kashmir but the whole valley turned into a place of hatred, Islamic fanaticism, rape, terror, arson, gruesome killings and kidnappings. The carnage of the innocent Pandits in Sangrampora, Chattisinghpora, Nadimarg, Wandhama, Gool and Chhanapora are not lesser in magnitude. Of the many, the gang rape of the nurse, Sarla Bhat, and her murder afterwards, and the rape and murder of the educationist, Girja Raina, are worse. Girja Raina was sawed into two pieces. On the night of January 19, 1990, announcements were made through loudspeakers in the mosques asking Kashmiri Pandits to leave Kashmir or else be prepared to die. In this frightful situation, the Kashmiri Pandits remembered how they had been hounded out of Kashmir six times in their history. This remembrance of the six migrations came alive. Once upon a time only eleven Kashmiri Pandit families had remained in Kashmir. The memory still sends a shiver down the spine of the Pandits who have been suffering from the persecution complex.

We find a subtle undercurrent of this feeling of insecurity in the literature written in exile especially the poetry. Maharaj Krishan

Santoshi, Hindi poet and short story writer, says: 'Kashmiri Pandit writers and poets took refuge in the Marxist ideology to hide this fear. They chose symbols which concealed their genuine feelings and, as such, did not express themselves openly.'

The shadow of this fear is still present in the Kashmiri writers. It is so because the readers of those exiled poets who write in Kashmiri are the Kashmiri Muslims. Yet, we continue to speak about uprootedness, nostalgia, loss of identity, preservation of cultural inheritance, complexity of new reality, refuge in the past, conflict, psychological dilemma, disgust, despair, hope, etc. This literature connects itself with the poetry of the Arab poets included in Abdullah-al-Udhari's *Modern Poetry of the Arab World.* The sensibilities of the Kashmiri Pandit writers resemble those of the Arab poets.

We have sown the seeds of Exile Consciousness Movement in Indian Literature. S S Toshkhani in his poem *Turning Back* hopes:

The memories of our home
are a half-forgotten song
that we hum all the while
and alone.
The way to our home
is through fire;
but it will not deter us
in that arduous adventure
which surely we shall undertake
one day.

Khema Kaul in her book *Samay ke Baad* paints two pictures of hopelessness and nostalgia:

> Darkness! Darkness! We are trying to know each other in this darkness. With smell! With touch! We ask for the road that leads to our home. We are petrified with our tongues stuck to the roof of our mouths. Darkness has spread over our being. It has enveloped us…
> And Vitasta! I see her all around without breaking her course.

Healthy like a pure Kashmiri woman! Robust! Oblivious of the whole world! She has got abundant love from the Himalayas. Vitasta! I salute you. I salute you from every side.

Things we left behind

Kirti Kaul

DARKNESS loomed large! Somewhere in the distance the voices grew louder, almost thunderously violent. The crowds swelled, the sounds rose, and the silence in the room deepened. In the smallest room of a large house, four benumbed bodies with shrivelled hearts and minds lay, overcome by the fear of the unknown.

In the quiet of the night, the rousing voices sounded louder, as the lashing of the tin drums began. I felt numb. Was it the chill of the night? I looked around the room to see if it was just me there to encounter three more faces staring into nothingness. Was it the quiet stillness of the room or the raging noise outside?

A small yellow bulb hung from the ceiling of the room making the pale faces look washed out. In the dim light they merged with the white walls of the room as the ghosts continued to haunt.

On a dark, wintry night it was not usual to perspire, but despite the chill in the air, I constantly wiped the watery droplets off my forehead, almost with a robotic efficiency. The door and the windows of this small room remained tightly shut, the air heavy and still.

This large house had seen some good times though. The garden that transformed its look each season—the light pastels of the spring, a wide variety of summer hues, the fiery orange of the autumn and the serene white of the winter. The gate at one end of the garden would open up into a vast field leading to the lake. A place where many of us often laid our worries to rest; its shiny, shimmering waters that reflected our true colours as it stood there, ever-inviting, just like a true friend. There were also those four Chinars on a mini island across the lake, unparalleled in their grace and splendour.

The beauty, the dignity, the colours, just everything around had now, however, been bludgeoned. The winter snow had smothered the greenery and the bloom of the sprawling garden outside, and its unguarded sprawl was fearful. Never before had the vastness of this house created such emptiness.

Normally abuzz with activity, the house was soaked in silence. It was no match for the loud voices outside. This was really our only refuge, or was it? We were not safe inside, and outside there was no guarantee.

It had been several weeks, the lines between friends and foes, trust and deceit, had blurred. Safe havens were no more. The brooks had stopped babbling and the waterfalls no longer made music. The city had transformed into a citadel with green flags, banners and posters ensuring that all other colours went unnoticed. No one paid heed to how quickly mornings gave into afternoons, and afternoons to evenings, and evenings into nights. The peace and the quiet of the nights had long exchanged their paths with sordid solitariness.

During the days the rising voices grew louder and louder, until that one morning when everything suddenly went quiet, quiet like the lull before the storm. This was not the peaceful quietude one yearned for. The silence was eerie, almost unbearable, so intense that one knew something was coming, and come it did.

It arrived early evening with the first announcement for the believers to gather. 'Perish, run or merge' the rest were told. For the voices on the loudspeakers there was no holding back. It was now or never. Voices changed, but the intent remained; we were being asked to leave the land which was ours.

Go, but go where? I asked myself. This was the only home I knew.

Evening slid into dusk, and retired into the night, but the voices did not tire; they continued to persist. It was then that we decided to move to the smallest room in the house—the room at the extreme end of the house, which in case of an intrusion, would be the last one to be spotted. Lines of anxiety crisscrossed my uncle's face. My aunt, normally a woman in charge of any situation, was visibly nervous. My cousin, who kept walking around almost compulsively, and me, with one question on our minds, 'will they come for us'?

In the past, the solitude that the night offered was always inviting, but this was one night I wanted to go away. By now the four of us had stopped talking to each other. There was no mention of dinner either, and even if someone was hungry, no one spoke of it. The night was still, but my mind continued to race with that one question. 'Will they come for us?'

No one knew.

The loudspeakers were now blaring, large crowds cheering at the lashing of the tin drums and announcements replete with hatred. There was yet another question to deal with now, 'when are they going to come for us?'

Pretty sure no one could help, I rolled up into a foetal position hoping for some divine intervention. The war between sound and silence seemed to be worsening, as my mind wandered to the lake outside. Its magnanimous depth, the wide expanse, the openness, the shimmering intensity, the lake stood as before, but...

Just when I thought I had made peace with fear, came the loud and clear, 'This belongs to us, not you.' For a moment I thought what I had heard couldn't be true, but within seconds came the next one, 'If you can't be one with us, get ready to flee or die.' Yes, we had heard it right. My uncle and aunt exchanged a frightened glance, trying hard to stay calm. After all, they had two young girls under their care and death wasn't the worst that could happen.

The frenzy continued; the voices on the loudspeakers were loud and clear. Wild cheering followed every slogan that was raised and hurled at us, the crowd endorsing it all. I shuddered, not sure if the confinement of the small room could save us at all. My uncle by now was the colour of ash. The fear of being surrounded was not distant anymore. The clarity with which the voice on the loudspeaker was inciting all those around was before us. The dissonance now had a pattern to it—the slogan on the loudspeaker, a wild endorsement from the mob and the ongoing lashing of the tin drums. In the silence of the room, death was palpable.

An occasional eye contact was all that there was. After all, there was really nothing to say. War between sound and silence, life and death, continued unfazed. Silence refused to die down, terrifying sounds just wouldn't go away, and life and death seemed to merge! There was nothing that the four of us could do, except lie frozen in time. Could I live with this?

Dawn was hours away, but would the sun really be able to bring my sunshine back?

No one quite realised when the bleak rays of the sun touched the mountains that lay across the lake. The weariness of the sleepless night lingered as everyone struggled to come to terms with the happenings of the last night. To me it all seemed surreal, quite like Dali's *The Face of War*. The fact that we were alive seemed untrue. The room bereft of any fresh air since the previous evening made no difference. In its smallness, the room continued to hold us, while we seemed to have fused with its stillness and staleness.

This tight rope walk between life and death made no sense, nothing made sense, even the fact that we were alive made no sense, and in those moments of senseless futility, it probably did not occur to anyone that we could actually open a window to let in some fresh air; possibly we continued to seek refuge in the stillness or was it that the stale air had befuddled us?

It was only by early afternoon that the blurred reality began to reveal itself. It was unimaginable that the four people in the room had not uttered a word over the last sixteen odd hours. Making a bleak attempt to move finally, my uncle got himself to open a window, and as I saw him walk towards the door, to me it seemed he was defying gravity.

That afternoon when I finally stepped out of the room, I knew I was walking into an unfamiliar world, a world that I knew little about, and in that moment I had also left behind something that was my own. Aware that what I thought and believed to be my own until yesterday was no longer mine, and if life could be frozen in frames, this is one moment I would choose to freeze.

The fact that we had not eaten anything since the previous evening was not really a concern at the moment, however, what next, though unspoken, was quite clearly a question we needed to figure out. Between the warring disconnect of the silenced house, and the noise raging inside our heads, clear answers were difficult to find, but I knew that movement was inevitable. Where that movement would lead us was something I could not foresee. All roads seemed to be leading towards the unknown and the unknown looked scary, at least in that moment.

Our minds seemed to fail us; we only had our instinct to rely on. Plenty of questions and no answers. It was difficult to escape from the whirlpool.

Knowing that it was time to move out of this house, and that we were lucky to survive the previous night, we made a hurried decision of taking me back to my parents, while my uncle and aunt along with my cousin would move out of the city until things settled a bit.

That was the last I saw of that house—my *matamaal* (maternal grandparents' house), the house where my grandparents had lived, a house that had sheltered me in my childhood pranks, a house where I had seen celebrations, some ordinary, others extraordinary. All I could carry back with me were the memories of the moments spent beside the lake overlooking the four majestic Chinars, the beautiful expanse of the lake with *shikaras* (boats) that seemed tiny in its generously large embrace, and of course the mountains in the background that stood guard in their pristine white.

By now, I wasn't sure whether I was happy about going back to my parents, or feeling sad driving away from the lake. After all, this wasn't my decision. Quite clearly I was being dragged away and that was not a good feeling at all. Hurriedly, my aunt packed some basic stuff as they readied to drop me back. The thought that we were not safe had not left us, and that made the journey even longer than the forty-five minutes it normally took. The city obviously had changed its cloak—gone was the simple beauty that was intrinsic to the lanes and by lanes, to the river that passed through the city, and the houses that lined up the river bank. Bridges that had once been the lifeline of the city and connected its core seemed to have gotten lost in the weary, wintry haze that seemed to have lost its sheen to the now established intolerance of the 'other'.

The city lived on, but its soul had been slayed.

Roads that had seen people brim with joy were now desolate. They now spoke stories of secrecy. Lanes bore testimony to murderous treachery, and by-lanes that held twists and turns in their narrow confines. Shops were conspicuous with their shutters shut. Fear and uncertainty made for a tasteless cocktail.

My presumption that meeting my family would reduce my worries was short- lived. One look at them and I knew that gloom had made its way here too. Nonetheless, even in times of despair, just being with my parents, siblings and my grandfather was a joy that was entirely mine to keep, something that remained untouched. It was no surprise, however, that overnight regular family conversations had been replaced by conversations around life and death. Fear had invaded our lives, and quite clearly it was here to stay.

Suddenly others made a demand for what I see, what I hear and what I wear. Never before had there been an expectation to wear my identity on my sleeve until now, and worse still, I had no qualms about my identity, rather I was quite proud of it, but for it to be made a 'condition' was unimaginable—my eighteen-year-old young mind could not tolerate it. Who could I direct my anger at? These were my own, gunning for all that I thought was mine as well, or at least something we could share, but was it, really?

Rumour mongering was the order of the day. I just could not fathom how a water pipe that bought water into our taps could only poison one and not the other. It was as if logic had evaded the frenzied minds totally. We had clearly gone way beyond any sense to prevail; even 'nonsense' would have made sense in such a situation.

Sagacity was lost!

That evening, my father did not come back home at the usual time. By eight it was unusually late for a person who lived his life between home and the hospital, tending to the sick. By ten at night we were paranoid, hoping against hope that he would come back home. What could we do—maybe lodge a missing person's complaint, but where and with whom? There was no one to reach out to.

Finally, by about 11.30 I saw my father walk in through the gate of our huge three-storied house that he had built with so much love and passion. He was visibly tired and walked as if in a daze. Seeing him, there was a sudden loss of emotion. If I had questions in his absence, his presence sought answers to those, and we knew this was going to be a difficult conversation to have; for us to ask the questions we didn't want to ask, and for him to explain his long absence.

He spoke in Kashmiri, a language we always conversed in, with a smattering of Urdu in a distinctly Kashmiri accent. As he spoke, we simply listened in silence. He had been bundled up, blindfolded, put into a jeep to attend to a wounded person. We knew, with the prevalent conditions, who the injured patients were, and any further questions were needless.

As he spoke, images of him in each of the situations ran before my eyes. The thought of him being home now evaded me completely, as the thoughts of what could have happened, had he not come back tonight raced across my mind. My mother was now worried, my eighty-five-year-old grandfather at a loss of words, and my young siblings sensing that nothing was quite all right, but oblivious to the gravity of the situation, and me trying hard to make sense of all that was happening around me.

Nothing was going to stop now; it was as if someone had blown away the beauty we were so proud of. It had disappeared, and gone into hiding! It wasn't going to be easy to look for it now. Frightful incidents continued to unfold, and we continued to live in terror.

At about 11 am, the next morning, the phone rang. The ringing of the phone was an ominous sign those days. In the last one month, it had only brought stories of death, decay and destruction. 'I believe your husband is involved in the renovation of a religious place,' the man on the phone spoke authoritatively. Holding the receiver in her hand, my mother froze. She could only blurt out a meek, 'Well, yes, but he doesn't mean any harm to anyone.'

'I understand, but he must refrain from it, times have changed, I hope you get it,' the male voice on the other end spoke again, and before my mother could respond, the phone was disconnected. This was enough for us to be shaken, and over the next few days the ringing of the phone became a norm.

Do you recognize the voice? Who could it be? What did it have to do with us, or even why us? We were asking too many questions, something we knew my mother had no answers to, no one actually did.

Pleasant conversations over the phone were a thing of the past. We now lived moment to moment; what would happen next was anyone's guess. We had been strictly instructed not to answer the phone when it rang, only my mother was allowed to do so. Day after day, the phone calls started coming, not one or two a day, but several, and this continued over a period of two weeks. Sometimes there was just silence at the other end. We were told that it was in our interest to leave. We were warned. From the bizarre to the ridiculous, we heard it all. Each time the voices were different, but there was one voice that my mother recognized, and we could only guess. I had heard people talk of fear, but never experienced it myself.

Over the next two weeks we attempted to behave like normal humans, as if nothing bad was happening. We did the basic cooking, cleaning and washing, but deep inside we all knew that this was not normal. What was normal though was deceit and treason. It was also normal to kill and raise slogans of all kinds. I was eighteen years old. The girl in me recognised the obvious lewdness in the slogans. My mind went back to the night at my uncle's house, 'after all death wasn't the worst that could happen'.

Fleeing was now inevitable! But where could we flee to, who would help us escape and just when should we, was all we spoke about. Our house could no longer offer protection. It was too huge for our small fears. Flurry of conversations followed; friends, relatives and families started checking with each other for passages to safety.

Children, women, old, disabled, sick people became categories to be transported. Fathers and sons prepared for separation, families were getting divided, friends had changed sides, chaos reigned supreme and it engulfed my family too.

My paternal uncle was the first to take the tough decision, deciding to move to a city in the vicinity. With three grown-up sons he felt that in a situation like this, he could take care of my grandfather, leaving my father to take care of his wife and three young children. That evening was not easy for us, and least of all for my father. My uncle arrived to take my grandfather with him and we did not know if we would see him again.

My father held his old father close, hugging him like he had never hugged him before, crying inconsolably. The tears lingered that night, no one slept, and no one said anything.

With grandfather gone, it was time for us to take a call. Where could we go? This was a difficult question to answer, but while we sought answers, we readied ourselves to leave what was our home. We packed some clothing, a few utensils and some of my books for the impending examination that the current situation had stalled. There was little money in the house, and going to the bank to withdraw some was impossible.

The larger question still remained unattended! Where do we go? Over the next few days, four families that included my maternal aunt and uncle's family got in touch with a friend in another city who helped them rent a small place. Money was sparse and had to be used discreetly for no one knew how long the journey would be, or what it would entail. With this sorted, finding a date and a time to leave was to be firmed up. The city was under siege; curfew had restricted all movement. Moving during the day was impossible and fleeing at night even worse. It was too much of a flux, too much for even the most sane to handle. The airport was the closest fleeing point for us, but getting there was not easy. With strict curfew imposed in the city, it would be difficult to reach anywhere unless we timed our departure impeccably. The day of departure finally arrived, preparations were completed the night before; one suitcase and two hand bags were all that we were taking with us, hoping that our going away would be only for a few months until the unrest settled.

That night, as we all lay down to rest, our minds and bodies, keenly aware that we were leaving our home behind became weary. A home where my siblings and I had spent our childhood, a home where we had dreamt of a lily pond with ducks around, a home whose produce from the kitchen garden made way into our food every day, a home that was made with the hard-earned money of two honest people who spent their life's earnings building it, a home where I caressed the dewy grass every morning, a home where the afternoon sun lit up the balcony railing, a home where the garden creeper offered a nest to the nightingales, a home whose walls echoed our childhood laughter and hid our pranks, a home that kept us warm in the winter snow, a home that had owned us, just as we owned it.

That home had to be left behind.

Left behind, but not forgotten. As I stepped out of the gate, I had no clue what was in store ahead. Was it a journey that had ended, or a journey that was to start. I did not know. What I did know was that while they could force us out of the city, they could never force the city out of us.

FICTION

I am from there. I am from here.
I am not there and I am not here.
I have two names, which meet and part,
and I have two languages.
I forget which of them I dream in.
—Mahmoud Darwish

Finger

Harikrishna Kaul

EGYPT Airlines took off from the Cairo airport at 10 in the morning. Majid sighed when he saw that his fellow passenger was a black. He thought, these blacks, rocks, trees, open fields, seas, animals, birds, whites and dark-skinned Indians will be there. And there will be the Kashmiri Pandit brother, Suman Dhar.

The plane had waited at the Dubai airport for two hours. Majid had liked the landscape, the lights and the skyscrapers. Accession of Kashmir to India had cost Majid much because the Indian passengers had to wait in the lounge for hours whereas the passengers from Jeddah to Karachi were allowed to board another plane and fly.

For Majid the people of Cairo looked like Kashmiris. The Nile reminded him of the meandering Vitasta of olden times. During the night he saw the beautiful Egyptian women swimming in the Nile. He recalled beautiful Kashmiri girls bathing in the Vitasta.

Majid did not visit the pyramids. He thought, they are meant for anthropologists. The Indian soldiers and the Afghanis made the Kashmiris dig graves everywhere. He loved the old city of Cairo and felt as if he had been walking through Nowhatta or Hawal in Kashmir. He saw the well-clad Egyptian schoolgirls carrying satchels. He saw some boys ogling and whistling at them. He saw signs reminding people of *namaz*. He saw air-hostesses in skirts. He heard of the cabaret dancers dancing in 5-star hotels and the drinkers revelling there.

The plane landed at the Accra airport in the evening. Majid collected his luggage and saw a Negro showing a placard with the words—Mr Abdul Majid Wani—written on it.

Majid said to him, 'I am Abdul Majid Wani.'

'Was the journey comfortable?'

'With the grace of God it was comfortable. What is your name?'

'Jacob. Sir, I welcome you on behalf of Sumaan Daar who is waiting for you outside. I will help you here at the counter.'

'Is he an agent of Robin and Richardson Company?'

'Sumaan Daar is the deputy project manager of the company.'

Majid understood now that it must be Suman Dhar, the knowledgeable boy in the engineering college at Srinagar. He had arranged a three-year contract, 3,000 dollars a month as salary, accommodation, medical facility and other things for Majid.

Suman Dhar embraced Majid. Both of them sat in the rear seat of the car. Majid asked Suman, 'Where are we to go?'

'The site is about 300 kilometers from here.'

'That is the distance from Srinagar to Jammu!'

'We will dine at an Indian restaurant. Are you from Hawal?'

'Yes, Hawal.'

'The restaurant is named Hawali. They serve dal, chappati,

kheer, puri, chicken biryani and shahi kabab.'

When they left the restaurant Majid thought the shahi kababs were tasteless.

They sat in the car.

Majid asked Suman, 'This black driver is…'

'His name is Kofi. He belongs to a very old race. They have their own culture and traditions.'

'What traditions? What culture? Cannibalism! '

'They name their children after the day they are born. This driver was born on a Friday. That is why he is called Kofi.'

'O, I see. Robinson Crusoe's assistant was called Man Friday.'

Both Majid and Suman laughed.

'Suman, you called me here. Why did you prefer me to others?'

'I told my company that I wanted an assistant to my liking for three months. They agreed. I talked to Ashok first but he doesn't have a passport. He gave me your telephone number.'

'Passport was an excuse. Ashok would not have come.'

'Why?'

'Ashok takes migrant salary in Delhi and works for a big company there. Freedom fighters and their jihad did nothing for Kashmiri Muslims. You Pandits benefitted from all this.'

'I phoned you when Ashok declined the offer.'

'And I came.'

'You had to come. What else could you have done? You are living in India. Right from 1988 you people used to cross the border and get training in handling weapons. Your salaries were paid to you regularly.'

Again they laughed.

Majid thought of the days spent in the engineering college in Kashmir when he, Ashok, and Suman were nicknamed the 'three musketeers' because they were always seen together.

'When will we reach the site? It is night,' Majid asked Suman.

'Soon. You need not worry. I have booked an apartment for

you. It has a fridge, an AC, television and other facilities.'

'Which flat do you live in?'

'I live in a bungalow with my wife. You will have lunch with us tomorrow.'

Majid had seen Suman's wife when they were married many years back. Suman was far away when Majid got married.

'It is dark. Where are we going? What desert are we passing through?' asked Majid.

'This car is plying on a road. Here are numberless trees. They are more in number than what one finds in the forests of Kashmir.'

'What trees are they?'

'I know only coconut trees. I can't name the other trees.'

'The sight of the sea tells me that I haven't divorced myself from the Wular, the Dal and the Manasbal lakes. The sound of water brings images of the Ahrabal waterfall and other streams. I feel that I am near them.'

'Don't be sentimental.'

And Majid rested his arm on Suman's shoulder.

'I am not sentimental. I am simply expressing myself.'

MAJID and Suman had lunch in a restaurant. Then Suman explained the complexities and subtleties of the project to Majid in his office. Suman said to Majid, 'Close these files now and come with me.'

'Dhar Sahab, what do you mean? It is early yet.'

Majid started addressing Suman Dhar as 'Sahab'.

'Don't worry, Majid. I told Eddy that we would leave by 3 pm.'

'Who is this Eddy?'

'He is the project manager. Our boss.'

'Why don't you address him as Sir?'

'Why? We don't speak even his full name.'

'What is his full name?'

'Edward Smith. No Sir or Mister.'

'These are bad manners.'

'No. It is love and intimacy. And don't call me Dhar Sahab. I am Suman.'

Kofi came with the car and took Majid to Suman's bungalow.

'Majid, this is my wife, Kiran.'

Kiran smiled and said, 'Namaskar.'

Majid looked at Kiran's face for a long time. He found her more beautiful than she had been in the eighties.

Majid looked at Suman and asked him a strange question, 'You Pandits match your birth charts and horoscopes before getting married. Who has matched the birth charts of you two?'

'That is known to Kiran. The parents of the girl get that done.'

'The match-maker must have been a poet. He has done a commendable job. The words Suman and Kiran rhyme. For him words and lives must have rhymed well.'

An eight-year-old handsome boy, with a satchel hanging from his shoulder, entered the room. He said 'Hello, uncle' to Majid and left. Suman said, 'This is our son Naigrai. Kofi collects him from school at 2 pm. When his lunch is over he studies in his room. Then he goes for swimming. On Sundays he plays golf in the club.'

Majid opened his bag and placed apples, walnuts and almonds on a table. Then he presented an embroidered shawl to Kiran. She ran her hand over the shawl and said, 'Thank you' to Majid.

Majid said to her, 'I knew that you would like the shawl.'

She said, 'I knew that you would come with a gift. But you did not get what I was expecting.'

'What?'

'*Haakh*.'

'I blame Suman for this. Had he given a hint on the phone I would have got it for you.'

The black African maid, wearing a blue and grey blouse, entered with the cups, tea kettle and snacks in a tray and placed them on the table. While taking tea Majid thought, had the maid not been black she would have been a very beautiful woman. Both were wearing lovely blouses. The arms of both were attractive. Kiran's arm was inviting. Such arms beautified Kashmir.

Kiran entered the kitchen and started talking to the maid. Majid and Suman left for a pleasure drive. Suman sat on the driver's seat and Majid sat by him. Suman said, 'Observe Africa.' Nothing seemed interesting or unusual to Majid. He thought, the trees are the same, the grass is the same, the bushes are the same and the roads are the same. Everything is the same.

Suman said, 'Majid, in school we thought that cannibals lived in Africa. I have seen some trees here which eat humans, animals and birds.'

Suman stopped the car, asked Majid to alight from it and walked him across the road. Majid felt fearful and said to Suman, 'I hope you won't take me towards that kind of tree and avenge the death of Tikka Lal Tapiloo whom the militants killed.'

Suman Dhar smiled, took Majid near the bushes, rested his left arm on Majid's shoulder and with the index finger of his right hand touched a leaf. The leaf shrank, folded, bent and then dangled from the branch. The same thing happened to the other leaves also that were near that leaf. Majid was terror-stricken. He remained silent. Suman read acute tension on Majid's face. He lifted his finger from the leaf. Slowly it came back to its normal shape.

Majid said to Suman, 'Is it touch-me-not flower?'

They sat in the car.

'The leaves are cowardly like Pandits,' said Majid.

'For me they are shy,' said Suman.

'Both mean the same thing.'

Majid saw a vast open field on the left. On the edge of the field there were three single-storeyed houses. Beyond them was the vast ocean.

Suman said, 'Look at the crows in the field. Their wings and heads are black. The chests and the necks are white. Look at this factory. It looks like the factory run by Qadir at Zaal Dagar.'

Majid looked at Suman's face.

Suman said, 'Why are you looking at me? The wealth of these people, like those of the Kashmiris, is the forests. The English looted their gold mines, made them slaves, took them across the Atlantic, sold them to the Americans and then took away the wood of their forests.'

'But we Kashmiris destroyed our forests ourselves.'

Suman stopped the car. Both came out and walked up to the bank of a stream. Suman took off his shoes and socks, rolled up his pants and walked into the water. Majid sat on a rock.

Suman said, 'Majid, my mother's parents lived in Baramulla. I used to visit them four or five times in a year. Recall Narabal and the road to Gulmarg. There is a stream called Ferozepur Nalla or Nalla Sukhnag where women fill their pitchers with water and wash clothes. They bathe and even swim in it. This stream looks like that stream. Pandits demand a homeland.'

Majid saw the liquid eyes of Suman. He diverted the topic by saying: 'We are late. Kiran must be waiting for dinner.'

Suman drove the car without stopping anywhere.

THE dining table looked very beautiful, very aesthetic. Majid could identify four dishes. Three dishes were Kashmiri. One of them was gushtaba. All the dishes were tasty. Majid felt happy at the hospitality of his friend. He said to Suman, 'All Pandits went beyond the mountains but you crossed the seas along with your wife Kiran and son Nagrai.' Then he looked at Kiran. He saw that her eyes were wet. He thought, What beauty! She reminds me of tragedy queens like Nargis and Meena Kumari. This family is rich.

Then he said to Suman, 'In three months I can earn so much…nine thousand dollars…it means lakhs of rupees.'

Suman said, 'You people also earn millions in Kashmir.'

'Yes, we can earn only when there is work. Work is possible if the funds are sent there. Everything is at a standstill there. I thank you for having called me here. You deserve praise for this.'

'I have only two friends. If I had a brother or a cousin I would not have asked you to come here.'

'We Kashmiris never discriminate. Isn't my brother your brother or your brother-in-law my brother-in-law?'

Majid looked at Kiran. She was wiping her tears with a hankie. Majid felt guilty and hung his head in shame. Sorrow was writ on Suman's face. Kiran stood up and left. Suman picked up a gushtaba and placing it on Majid's plate said, 'Eat it. Even Pandits can cook gushtabas. Don't pay attention to anything. Kiran becomes sentimental at times.' Majid ate a piece of gushtaba and did not relish it this time. He thought, Did this Pandit woman consider me wicked? Her beauty has cast a spell on me. But that doesn't mean that I can misbehave with her.

Suman offered a Punjabi dish to Majid. He ate it and then looked at his watch. He stood up, washed his hands and wiped them with a napkin. He shook Suman's hand and said: 'Thanks for this excellent dinner.' He was about to leave when Kiran came smiling and asked him to have ice cream or coffee. Majid said to her, 'No, I've had enough.' Then he thought: I ate humiliation.

THREE months went by. With them was over the three-month contract of Majid. He never went to Suman's place in these three months. Majid just listened whenever Suman talked about his personal and private affairs. A number of times he thought of forgetting the unpleasant situation but the recollection of Kiran's tears pained him.

It was 4 in the morning. Majid was waiting for the car that would take him to the airport. The car came. Instead of the driver Suman was in it. He came out of the car and picked up Majid's suitcase and bag. Majid snatched the luggage from Suman's hands and kept it in the luggage compartment of the car. He sat on the seat beside Suman. Suman said to Majid, 'This road leads to the famous rainforest in Africa. It is a dense forest of trees which are taller than the pine trees. Ropes have been tied from one tree to another for transporting things. From the rope even a weak-hearted person can see the whole forest. It is dawn. When you came here it was night. What happened to you on the first day when Kiran wept and left the dining room? Why did you feel insulted?'

'I did not feel insulted. I cursed myself. I was to say: Had you given this job to your brother or brother-in-law I would have been happy but due to a slip of the tongue I said, your brother is my brother and your brother-in-law is my brother-in-law. Kiran must have thought, I meant to say: Your wife is my wife. Am I so wicked to entertain such mean and low thoughts?'

'My brother-in-law… I mean… Kiran's brother Sanjay was killed by the militants on the eighth of March in 1990. First, his eyes were pulled out. Then bullets were showered on him. When you talked about him twice you actually showered bullets on Kiran.' Majid embraced Suman, and both of them wept.

'Convey my apologies to Kiran. Tell her that my two cousins were also killed in the same way. Mushtaq got killed in a cross-fire in Maisuma. Basharat, who was engaged to my younger sister Jameela, came to Kashmir from Kanpur. When he reached there he disappeared. Nothing is known about him. Either the Indian army thought that he was a Pakistani agent and killed him or militants considered him an informant of the Indian army and killed him. Jameela is still waiting for him. Mother has gone mad.'

Suman said, 'It is morning. These are the bushes that I showed you on the first day when you came here. They shrink and bend out of fear or shyness like Pandits. Touch a leaf before you leave this place.'

'It is one thing to touch something with your finger, another thing to show your finger and quite another thing to fool a person. Someone showed you Pandits a finger or a hand and you shrank like a touch-me-not flower. My dear brother, outsiders as well as our own people fooled us... I mean... fingered us. Pakistan and India cheated us. Suman, even away from home you are free like an ocean. I too have a home and have to go a long way to reach there. Ultimately I have to go there. I want to reach the airport in time.'

Suman opened the doors of the car. Both of them sat in it. They did not talk. Suman drove the car.

(Translated from Kashmiri by Arvind Gigoo)

The rented house and the flat

Henna Koul

IT has been over twenty-one years since I left my rented house and shifted into my own flat. These years have passed restlessly, abandoned and deserted. Nightmares, the cries and wrinkled faces followed me everywhere. I was left bewildered and clueless. I used to wake up every midnight and have glimpses of the faint eyeballs and parched lips. They used to appear at midnight and disappear in the morning. I packed my clothes and came out of my house. I did not know where to go. But I went to the railway station, bought a ticket and boarded a train. Random images of episodes appeared. I thirsted for water. The train stopped at the next station and I got off. A horse cart driver urged me to sit in it. I was wondering where I was to go. Whenever I closed my eyes, unorganised pictures appeared and I saw the vision of the faint eyeballs and parched lips. An old woman waved and showed direction to the cart driver. The road was in a dilapidated condition. I asked the cart driver to stop but he ignored me. Finally he dropped me at a place and left in a hurry. Just as I stepped down, a half-clad kid caught me. He took me to a house.

The house stood on pillars. The room was full of cobwebs. Old paintings were partially visible. The kid freed my hand and went to one of the corners of the room where there was an old locked rusty trunk. The clock was ticking. There was a loud thud when the bulb exploded. The kid vanished. I was surrounded by people. They were congratulating one another. I flipped another leaf of the album. There was more lightning and thunder. There was complete confusion because people were running here and there. They looked at the man who had been shot. They saw the man dying. Nobody came forward to help. Later, the body was taken by his wife and two kids. At another place a body was beheaded. I, along with my family members, hid in the room. Silence prevailed everywhere. Even a knock on the door frightened us. Nobody dared open the door. We heard footsteps and loud shrieks. We did not understand what was happening. Gunshots were heard.

My grandmother gathered the strength to open the door. To her amazement it was a neighbour. The neighbour said to her, 'Pack up and leave as soon as possible. They beat him and finally shot him. They will not leave us too. Our sons' names appear in the hit list. I heard two young boys talking to each other. They pointed towards our house. They were holding guns.'

My grandmother said, 'Are you mad? It might be your illusion. Our friends gave us assurance that we would be safe here.'

My neighbour said, 'I followed the young boys silently and saw them beating him. They dragged him out of the house, beat him in front of the mob and finally killed him. We are not safe here. It is high time we moved from here otherwise we are doomed. Think of your children and grandchildren.'

The same night we again heard knocking at the door. I drew the curtain to see who it could be. It was the neighbour again. Quickly he opened the door and bade goodbye to us.

I flipped another page of the album. I was in a dilemma. My parents were packing and putting things into a trunk. I thought of my room, my comic books, my toys, my friends, my freedom. A mirror fell off the wall and broke into pieces. I went near the shattered pieces and saw myself, my parents and my grandparents scattered. I was silent.

I heard a voice. It was a young girl. She took me out of the house. I was made to walk through many villages. I was directed towards unfamiliar hilly areas and plains. I reached a place surrounded by mountains. It gave me a momentary pleasure. I yearned for my roots and peace of mind. The kid took me to a room. As I entered the room the child vanished. I was motionless. I felt something moving around. I realised that the room housed scorpions and lizards. As I flipped another leaf of the album, the hazy photographs and images of people were there. The faces were blank and the minds confused. Their movements, actions, thoughts and words seemed impaired. There was contradiction in their thoughts and actions. The memory faded. They showed signs of decay, dementia and aloofness. Slowly I observed that something was going wrong. The elders in the family were feeling uprooted. Loss of identity and memory, mental agony, and disinterestedness constituted their lives. They remained engrossed in their own imaginary world. As I was looking at the photograph an elderly man came.

He said, 'What has brought you here? Why did you come here to disturb us? What do you want from us?'

I said, 'A small child directed me to come here. Why are you angry? What did I do? I took care of you.'

He replied, 'You took care of my physical being and gave me

medicines, interacted with me, helped me in every way. You were there when I needed you. But did you take care of my mental pain, my distress, my loss of interest, my struggle with the new environment, loss of memory and identity? Where were you for all these years? Did you ever long for me as I long for my own home?'

With a flash of light, an elderly woman appeared. She was in anguish. She said, 'I always longed for a social circle, your company and your conversation. You were engrossed with your own being and your work. You forgot about us. You stopped talking to us as you grew up. You used to fight with me. You left me the moment I needed your presence. I longed for your presence. I loved you and this was what I received. I was struggling with my life for days together. I thought that you would come to see me.'

The man and woman in the photograph grasped my hand. I shrieked but I wasn't able to hear my voice. They said, you forgot about us. We did not expect this from you at all. We are alone in this old age. We have no one to talk to, no one to share our feelings with.'

I felt shattered. I bent down on my knees. I flipped another leaf of the album. I saw a shadow. I recognised this shadow. It was the same shadow that had left me years ago. It stood before me. It voiced, 'So dear, you are back. I had asked you not to leave them… but you had your own aspirations, desires and dreams to realise. Why are you back now? What made you come here? No one needs you now.'

I said, 'Do you think I am responsible for it?'

The shadow said, 'I had asked you to think before leaving this place, this home and this family.'

The tale of the Satisar

Chandrakanta

THERE is Kathabab, Pandit Krishan Joo Kaul's house. Hey Shankar! There is nothing left here except a pile of broken bricks and burnt and corroded bits of the roof. So has this house also been sacrificed? The house is empty. After the death of Krishan Joo Kaul and Saraswati, Bhadra, Nathji and Indira also left. Death engulfed the house. It is not likely to spare anyone.

Raja hasn't returned. Babboo is a bank officer posted somewhere in Bhadarwah or Kishtwar. It seems Sangeeta and children are in Jammu where Sangeeta has a job.

Nathji's daughter Neelam has chosen to be alone. She lives with Dr Katyayini in Shihul Villa. She spends all her time taking care of the patients. She hasn't married. She has no family. What about that doctor who used to daydream and call Neelam,

'Neelmaal fairy'? Who knows where he is? Does he still remember Neelam?

Here we are at Shihul Villa. The house and the hospital look the same as they did ten years ago, just a little dirty and depressing. The walls are a little damp because of the melting snow. The slogan—Anyone who fears Allah should pick up a Kalashnikov—written on the wall of the house has faded away.

But even two years after his death it is impossible to forget Omkar bhai. Upon seeing the slogan written on the wall of the house, he had lost his temper. He had tried to wipe it off the wall. Two days later, he was found dead on the road. The terrorists had cut off his hands.

Katya and Kartik are sitting close to the *bukhari* for warmth. Sati and Neelam are working in the kitchen. Sati now speaks much less than she did before. The house feels ghostly without the children. Isha is in Delhi. Tipu is working in Bombay. What will the house be like once Sati goes away to stay with her son? Katya doesn't want to think about it.

Omkar continued to be Katya and Kartikeya's son even after he became a father. Kartik has also become like blue-throated Shiva who drank poison. He can't talk about Omkar nor can he forget him.

'Let me check my e-mail till the food is ready.' Katya gets up and goes into the computer room. Arjun and Alka are in America. They may have sent a mail.

She downloads the e-mail. There are two or three messages.

'We are fine, mum. How is Dad? There is good news for you. Alka is carrying.'

Dr Arjun has sent the news from Illinois that Kartik and Katya are about to become grandparents. True? Eight years after their marriage? Kartik will be overjoyed. Katya is happy.

The second message: 'Lalli is not doing too well.' Nandu from New Jersey.

A shadow passes over Katya's face.

'Kartik! Ma isn't well.' Her voice is shaking.

'What is the matter? Come here, let us talk.' Kartik puts his arm around her.

'I don't think Ma will be able to wait any longer. Should we send Isha to her grandmother?'

'Come on. Don't be silly. Ma is old now; her health will go through some ups and downs. Let her get a little better and then we can go ourselves and bring her back with us.'

Kartik knows how to soothe wounds.

'I couldn't fulfill my promise, Kartik. I wanted to bring Lalli back to Vishnu Vatika one more time. At this stage of life one relives and remembers past friendships, relations as well as the time spent in one's home.'

'You are right, Katya! For a while it seemed as though things were improving. But militancy has increased again after the Kargil war. Nandu knows that. I am not sure whether Ma will be able to endure such a long journey now.'

Katya is sobbing with her head on Kartik's shoulder.

Why is this brave doctor's heart melting like this?

Is it because she could not fulfill the promise she had made to her mother? Or is it because, despite living with her own family in an alien land, Lalli has continued to yearn for the fragrance of her own home and its surroundings? She has never been able to forget Reshi Pir, Chrar-e-Sharif, Shankaracharya Temple and Tulla Mulla Mandir.

She still dreams of the lofty peaks of Vishnupad.

Katya is saddened by the fact that she could not justify her mother's faith. She had told her mother, 'Lalli, history is a witness that we survived even after being reduced to only eleven families. We gradually grew into a community of thousands and created a new history. You will see that your Katya will also be a part of those eleven families.'

Neelam and Sati have laid the food.

Someone is knocking at the door.

'Who is it?'

'Ghulam Rasool, doctor sahib.'

'What is it, Ghulam Rasool, at this time of night?'

'There is an emergency case, sahib. Yusuf's daughter is in great pain...'

'Oh God ! What happened?'

'Even four women can't handle her. She has bloodied herself hitting her stomach. She says she doesn't want a militant ...'

'Inform Dr Kiran and Dr Shamim. They should prepare for a surgery. I will follow.'

Dr Katya pulls her coat over her shoulders and walks with Ghulam Rasool towards the emergency ward. Even Dr Kartikeya cannot stop Katya nor does he try. Yususf's daughter, who is a victim of the terrorists, is under Katya's care. She is eight months pregnant. Katya will have to operate.

LET us go towards the lake now. The scene here is very upsetting. There is Khurshid's elder son and Ali Joo's houseboat. Would it be bad manners if we took a peep inside?

Ali Joo is sitting on a carpet made in Anantnag and smoking his hookah. He has grown quite old. There are hardly any tourists nowadays. One sees just a handful of them during summer. After the incident when terrorists killed six tourists in a houseboat, all the visitors avoid staying in the houseboats.

Ali Joo's sons have now joined their cousins' business. They sell handicrafts in an emporium in Delhi. They even go to Goa to sell their merchandise. Ali Joo's son Saif has even constructed a house on the Delhi-Haryana border. It is true that Ali Joo felt strange that day as though his son was becoming a foreigner. The only consolation is that he comes home frequently. Saif has said clearly, Now we should consider Hindustan as our country, Baba. And like our Pandit brothers, we should get into the habit of tolerating the heat and humidity of the plains. Otherwise we will continue to behave like frogs in a well. There aren't enough jobs for everyone in the valley. It is better to make an effort on one's own rather than wait for government help. India is a large country after all. Our destiny is linked to it. Even today, there are thousands of young men who are jobless in Kashmir. There won't be any miracles even if new policies are formulated. So, we have to move out and look for opportunities.

Actually the militants have driven Saif crazy with their demands for money. Rehana and Jawahra are also growing up. He is worried about his family. Who knows when someone will leave a packet of henna on their doorstep?

But how can his old father find any solace in the sunset of his life? He is not prepared to leave his house, his houseboat or Mazar Bal.

And in the meanwhile, he waits for tourists to arrive.

THIS is Mangala mausi's house in Chanpora. She passed away long ago. Now her son Ajay and his wife Shobha live in the house. Her grandson Vicky is in Hyderabad. Shilpi is in Chandigarh with her husband. They keep getting transferred. The elders are destined to be lonely. Most of the Pandits in the valley have sent their children and grandchildren away. They don't have the right to play with the future of their children because of their love for their own home. It doesn't matter what happens to them.

Ajay is sitting in the dark dispensary, waiting amidst medicines, bottles, jars, old and new instruments and assorted stuff. Who is he waiting for? For patients or friends? Or just so that he can exchange a few words with someone. Ajay and Shobha live in apprehension, afraid of those frightening voices that startle them within and outside the house. Sometimes Shobha says, 'God knows why we are here. What are we waiting for? I am longing for the children…'

Vicky had asked his father, 'Why are you still holding on to this house now, Papa? You are constantly balanced on the edge of fear all the time! You can't even talk freely to anyone. You don't know when an enemy will suddenly raise his head! Why don't you listen to me, sell the property and come and live with me?'

'Look!' Ajay became philosophical as he peered through the gloom, 'Whatever happens is the will of God.'

'The will of God or your politicians?'

Ajay is quiet. He wishes he could peek into the future. In the meanwhile, the shop is open. Trigami Sahib is coming. He has always had bad teeth. Ajay doesn't take any money from him even today. It is enough that at least someone comes and exchanges a few words with him in this wilderness. A veil of secrecy has fallen over Khudai Manzil, the home of Rehmanjoo's sons. The Border Security Force keeps a watch on visitors to the house. Shabir is linked with the freedom movement. He hopes to become the leader of the state one day.

THE place is Jammu. We see Trikuta Nagar. There is the home of Keshavnath Raina. No, it is Premji's house. Keshavnath is not alive any more. Kamala also passed away two months after his death. They suddenly discovered that she had cancer in the last stage. Katya, Kartikeya had come to meet Lalli and Premji after they were released by the militants. Lalii hugged her daughter and son-in-law for a long time.

'Where did those brutes touch you? Lalli will wash away the scars with her blood and tears.'

'No, Lalli. They really had taken us to treat some of their injured companions. They didn't misbehave with me. They were scared themselves.' Kamala couldn't believe it.

'How can anyone believe that animals that can cut a woman into two would ever let Katya go without misbehaving with her?'

She wept as she spoke.

'You are right, Kakini. Anything could have happened to me but they needed me for other reasons. And even if something of the sort had happened to me it would only have been a terrible episode. The greatest sorrow and pain that I suffered was my worry for Kartikeya...'

Katya's voice became gruff with tears. Kamala hugged her, crying loudly.

'You have come back to us, child. We don't want anything else.'

Nandan-Dhara had come and taken Lalli away with them to New Jersey a year after Keshavnath's death.

'Don't worry about Dulari and Katya, Lalli! I will always be there for them,' Prem had reassured Lalli as she departed.

'Go, travel a little and then come back. Sharika's sons Aniruddh and Arvind are in Washington. You should spend a few days with them. You must visit Arjun as well. He is in Illinois. You won't even realise how time passes.'

Vijaya cried. Bulbul is working in Bangalore. Pamposh has settled in Pune after marrying a Marathi boy. Lalli's presence was like a benign, cool shade. How is Vijaya going to stay alone in the house now?

Prem is surrounded by friends and acquaintances as usual. He is preoccupied with so many problems—the problems of the entire community and the problems of the migrants. There are worries of getting no relief or help from the government agencies.

Premji is associated with many relief organisations.

The houses of many migrants have been burnt down. Some of them are not getting their salaries while the pensions of others have been stopped.

Problems related to the schooling of children, medicines for elders, the hope of going back home, the eagerness to re-connect with what they have left behind! And the demand for *Panun Kashmir* (Our Kashmir) is growing louder and louder.

Rattan Warikoo still cannot forget Syed Shahabuddin's statement, 'Kashmiri Pandits betrayed the trust of the Kashmiri Muslims by migrating on the advice of the Governor and they started a propaganda campaign which became the root cause of terrorism…'

Great, Shahabuddin Sahib! That was well said! It was merely on the provocation of the Governor that Kashmiri Hindus abandoned their homes and properties worth crores of rupees and came to live in tents and hovels, penniless and destitute! What amazing logic!

'Let it be, Rattan bhai. Shahabuddin Sahib's house is safe. It is only the homeless, living under the naked sky who feel the pain of losing their homes. Ask Behal Saqi in Delhi who says: "Losing your home is like climbing on to a pyre or lying down in a grave while you are alive. Only someone who has lost a home can appreciate the real meaning of home."'

(Translated from Hindi by Ranjana Kaul)

A tale of the animals

Moti Lal Kemmu

AND then the next day, curfew was imposed in Vananchal and the animals fell silent. After two days, when the curfew was relaxed for a few hours, posters were found pasted on trees warning the hangul and deer to leave Vananchal forever. The wolves had taken the responsibility of terrorising and killing some hangul and deer.

Upon seeing the deteriorating state of affairs, the violent atmosphere, the bloodshed, and the collapse of law and order in Vananchal, the authorities changed the governor of the forest. A new phenomenon unfolded. Unknown animals started setting everything on fire. The sacked governor made a fiery speech and held the central government responsible for the mess. He made a startling revelation that a huge quantity of arms and ammunition had been smuggled from across the border to fuel the mayhem. Jackals were actively involved in killing others. The former governor held the armed forces deployed on the border responsible for the hopeless situation.

The new governor clearly stated that necessary steps would be taken to eliminate those spreading terror in Vananchal. His speech, which was full of warnings, was aired on the radio.

After two days, when the curfew was lifted for some hours, a jackal attacked some deer while they were on their way to the bank of a river to quench their thirst. When the deer fell down, the jackal shouted: 'This is your fate, you informants. To die. Leave Vananchal immediately or else face the consequences. This place is ours.'

Such killings of innocent animals forced the new governor to put the whole of Vananchal under curfew for an indefinite period. In spite of the curfew one could sense the frantic movement of animals in the nooks and corners of the forest. During the curfew relaxation period, the jackals protested against the high-handedness of the administration. Newspapers carried the pictures of those deer that had been killed by jackals. Soon, the tone of editorials and write-ups changed. One could sense that the newspapers were under threat too. The deer and hangul were warned and asked to leave Vananchal. The carcass of a prominent deer, a leader, was found by police personnel and then cremated.

In the area inhabited by the jackals there was widespread resentment and anger against the imposition of curfew. There were strict restrictions on their movements. But they also hit upon alternative ways to circumvent any restrictions. They got wolves, bears and foxes together, and came out in hordes to announce their intent. Voices were heard all over Vananchal. 'Vananchal will be free.' When the authorities arrested Gidad Joo, the leader of the jackals, the jackals got angry and set fire to the trees. Some jackals took revenge by killing some more deer.

In this chaos, nobody knew how many deer and hangul got killed and how many fled Vananchal.

An old jackal lived alongside the deer and hangul. The jackal visited the deer at night and asked them to flee Vananchal because they were not safe there any more. 'Save your lives,' said the old jackal to the deer. 'Don't trust us. The days of living in harmony and peaceful co-existence are gone. Our leaders are dangerous. You will be killed if you stay here. Your fodder will be burnt. Your caves will be destroyed. Remember, you are the minority. You will be wiped out in no time. If you want to save your lives, run away from here. Leave Vananchal to the jackals. No one will save you. The authorities have become corrupt. They will side with the jackals…' The old jackal went on and on.

On hearing the words of the old jackal, a young deer addressed others, 'We can run away. But can we tolerate the pain and pangs of leaving our Vananchal? This forest is ours. We have been living here for centuries much before the jackals came into the picture. The wolves and jackals want our ouster.'

'Don't be emotional,' said a skinny deer. 'If we want to save ourselves we must run away from Vananchal. This place has already been snatched from us. It has been taken over by hungry jackals from the forest nearby. We are too puny to put up a fight. Don't you see we are being hunted down one by one? Those who left didn't talk to others about it. They did not even confide in others. They just bundled their belongings and ran away quietly…'

'If we survive, we can come back,' said the deer in a chorus. 'But for now, we must not wait…'

While the hangul and deer were debating whether to flee Vananchal or not, a sound blared. Shoon, shoon, shoon… Everyone was startled and afraid. The deer and hangul fell silent. After some time when the hangul and deer mustered the courage to check what was going on, they saw the old jackal lying in a pool of blood. He was trembling. Life was oozing out. 'They shot me…the wild beasts came and did this to me,' the dying jackal cried, 'see what they have done…O God…'

'The old jackal has been killed,' an old deer whispered in fear, 'This is the final warning…'

A young deer read the message that had been written on the bark of a tree next to where the old jackal lay dead: 'We will kill all informers. The old jackal was an informer. We are fighting for freedom and the old jackal was supporting the hangul and deer.'

The young deer whispered to the others, 'If this is the fate of a jackal, what will be ours?'

Sometime later, a speeding police vehicle stopped abruptly near the Deer-Hangul lane. Three police personnel took the body of a young hangul out of the jeep and placed it on the ground. Soon after, they left. The deer and hangul watched in horror. Even the hangul working for the Government weren't safe.

The same night, when the deer and hangul were awake in their caves, loud voices were heard all across Vananchal.

He will come and get us freedom.
He who will be called *Sarhadi*, he will sacrifice his life.
High-handedness of the authorities will not be allowed.
This government is a government of slaves.
We need a free government, our own government.
We have nurtured Vananchal with our blood.
This Vananchal is ours.
Today or tomorrow, we will get our freedom.
You deer and hangul, leave our Vananchal
While there still is time, leave Vananchal.

For the whole night, the voices blared spreading terror and fear. Herds of deer and hangul started to leave Vananchal for alien forests. The next morning, the forest was burning. The jackals and wolves captured the caves of deer and hangul.

Years later, when there were no deer and hangul left in Vananchal, the jackals and wolves asked the same question over and over again: 'Why did the deer and hangul run away from here?'

(Translated from Hindi by Tej K Zadoo)

Akanandun

Maharaj Krishen Santoshi

IN the folktale, when after twelve years the Yogi comes, the mother becomes sad. She curses the moment when she had accepted the Yogi's condition. That time she had been desperately yearning for a son. The Yogi had blessed her with a son but had set one condition.

What condition?

That her son will remain with her for twelve years only…

And after that?

After that, he will have to be returned to the Yogi.

Hearing the Yogi's condition, husband and wife had become sad. Both had vacillated between 'Yes' and 'No'.

'We accept it,' they had said together after a long pause. All they wanted was a son. And Yogi had granted them the boon. But the Yogi's condition was that the child had to be returned to him.

MOTHER liked to listen to the story of Akanandun a lot. Ghulam Mohammad Dar had sung it in his sweet voice. Every now and then, mother would ask me to write a letter to Radio Kashmir to broadcast the song. Whenever it was broadcast, she would leave aside all her work and listen to it with attention. Sometimes, I would also be with her. During those times, she would truly become the mother of Akanandun and I would become Akanandun in my imagination.

Mother, the Yogi has come, I would say.

Go and hide somewhere, Akanandun! I will tell the Yogi that you have gone to visit your maternal grandparents.

There was turbulence in mother's tone.

Why so, mother? I asked in surprise.

I cannot tell… (aside) No, no, I will not hand you over to the Yogi! You are mine now. I will not give you back to the Yogi.

Here, the Yogi was making appeal after appeal.

Where is Akanandun? Call him quickly. Give him to me. I have come to take him back…

Mother became helpless. She, along with her husband and Akanandun, came out of her room.

The Yogi pulled Akanandun towards him.

I am hungry, the Yogi said to Akanandun's mother.

Vegetables and rice are ready, Yogi Maharaj, said the mother.

No, I want meat.

Please forgive us, Yogi Maharaj. From where will we get meat at this hour?

I want the meat of your son.

O God! What are you saying, Yogi Maharaj!

The voice of the mother was drowned in grief.

In the folktale, mother and father under compulsion kill their son, cook his meat in a big pot, and place the meat in four plates. One plate is for the Yogi. Two plates are for the mother and father. The fourth plate is for Akanandun.

Go, call Akanandun, the Yogi said in a commanding tone.

Akanandun! Akanandun! the mother called in a hoarse voice.

Coming, mother... It was Akanandun's voice.

When mother turned around to look, the Yogi was nowhere nor were the plates seen.

After the exodus, mother had forgotten even Akanandun. In the alien city with its blazing sun, it looked as if the tender spots of the place had dried up. In whichever direction she looked, only dust, smoke, and thorny bushes were seen. Mother felt helpless looking out of the window. Whenever she looked out of the window she trembled. That is why I had forbidden her to look outside.

One day, I said to her: Come, mother, let me tell you Akanandun's story.

Do you want to make me cry, mother said laughingly.

No, mother. It is not like that.

I was joking. Okay, tell me. Let me see if you know the art of storytelling or not.

Mother sat down. And I started narrating the story.

I began:

Mother, this time it so happened that before the Yogi's return Akanandun was killed. He had gone to the market to buy a few things for his twelfth birthday. Perhaps some envelopes from the post-office! The letters were to be written to those friends who had migrated. But Akanandun didn't return home to his mother and father. He died in a grenade blast. His mother wept bitterly. In a few days the Yogi was to come. What would she tell the Yogi? How would she return what was entrusted to her? No, no, she would not be able to show the Yogi her face. She would go somewhere and hide. Her husband had already faded. Now even the son had been killed. No, no, she would not live here now. I will jump in the river, she thought.

Where did Akanandun's mother go? Nobody knows.

Hand-grenades were exploding in the city. Soldiers were deployed. On the roads, the hustle and bustle was not as it used to be. Twelve years ago, when the Yogi had come to this city, it was peaceful. Smiles shone on people's faces. The rivers, weather, and the greenery were beautiful. Now one was scared of one's own shadow. Stench of rotten meat emanated from everywhere. Although the Yogi was wearing wooden clogs, he was walking at a brisk pace. When he reached Akanandun's home, he was surprised to see a padlock hanging from the door. Until then, such a thing had never happened. Some inauspicious thing had surely happened. The atmosphere of the city was bad. The city had become a capital of mourning. Screams were coming out of the half-burnt houses. Has some demon come to the city and caused so much destruction?, thought the Yogi. Has Akanandun's family also perished in this destruction? But the padlock on the door conveyed that the people of the house had fled somewhere out of fear.

The Yogi had come walking a long distance. He was tired and wanted to rest. He lay down on the little patch of green turf. He fell asleep. He would have continued sleeping had he not felt some hard object jab into his body. He got up agitated. Some soldiers surrounded him. One soldier with a gun in his hand shouted at him, who are you and what are you doing here?

I am a Yogi.

If you are a yogi, what is your work in this terror-stricken city?

I have come here after twelve years. I don't know anything else.

Then you go back, the soldier mocked.

Where shall I go? How shall I go unless Akanandun returns home?

There was pity in the Yogi's voice.

Then stay in a prison until that time. We will help you reach there.

Other soldiers guffawed together. Amid this sound of collective laughter, one soldier's commanding voice rang out: The evening is coming. You find your shelter, Yogi.

Shelter! Shelter!

The Yogi laughed at the words uttered by the soldier. So much power emerged from his laughter that the soldiers left without arguing further.

During the night the Yogi returned to Akanandun's home. The padlock on the door was there. A weak light was straining out from the nearby houses. He came near the door and shaking the padlock he started calling: Akanandun! My Akanandun! Where are you?

He continued calling for a long time but not even a window opened. It was a moonlit night and in this moonlight he saw the face of a woman through the window of a house nearby. The woman beckoned the Yogi to come close to her house.

Then she whispered: Please be silent, Yogi. My son is sleeping. Today after two years he has been released from jail. He fell asleep just now. Don't wake him up with your hue and cry. I request you, please go away from here.

There were tears in the woman's eyes. Her voice was hoarse.

But, where is my Akanandun? asked the Yogi in a pitiable tone.

Your beloved Akanandun has been killed. He will never come back now.

And his family?

Don't know. Now, Yogi, please go away and do not return to this place.

There was irritation in the woman's tone. The Yogi respected the feelings of the woman and left.

In the morning, on the bank of the lake, he was found dead.

You are listening, aren't you, mother?

(Translated from Hindi by Sualeh Keen)

The shadow

Autar Krishan Rahbar

I read the news; then read it again. Read it a third time. It was an interesting piece of news. I wished I could smile but I only wondered at the events and happenings. I hurriedly glanced over the newspaper, read some more news items and came out of the Government Library.

One news item stuck to my mind. I felt tired—the road lengthened and a different thought occupied me—the thought of my landlord who had served me a verbal ultimatum to vacate the house I was living in, latest by the end of the month, which was approaching fast. A house? A house indeed! A box-like construction, two rooms of a single-storey building, a tiny kitchen and a small bathroom sandwiched between the two. In fact, a modest Delhi flat—a place to suffer the pain of living there and the pain of memories of my own home and land left in Kashmir. With a fixed income and spiralling rent and no extra rupee to spare, it was a life of torture. In a short span of time I had changed three houses after suffering the humiliation of being banished from my homeland.

Finally, I had arranged a meeting with a property dealer who had fixed the date for the meeting today. This was the first meeting. Earlier he had fixed a house for me, but then, after close scrutiny the owner had changed his mind. He was convinced that I had a bigger family than his house could accommodate. At another place the owner did not like the fact that I was a non-vegetarian. Though I offered to abstain from non-vegetarian food, he was not ready to trust me. The third landlord wanted a tenant of his own caste, and it was not possible to change my caste. So things did not materialise. But, who knows, this time there may be luck in store for me! What a struggle, what a shame! This thought made me walk faster. My shadow followed me as usual, but now, when I was running, my shadow came closer to me and stuck to my right side. The shadow changed shapes. Now like a cow, and now a calf. It was tortuous. I dragged my feet that constantly pained me. The flesh had stuck to the hot metalled road. I perspired badly, and worse still, wiped the sweat off with my dirty handkerchief. I noticed that my shadow had fossilised.

In the last five years, after my migration from Kashmir, I must have consumed quintals of dust off the wide and long roads of Delhi. Burnt dust, sand and my sweat, together produces a nasty and repelling smell. On such a sultry day, the only escape is a bathroom. I would usually lock myself in the bathroom and stay there. And in the bathroom I would dream of shining silvery drops of the bright, cool water of Kashmir, shadows of a Chinar and the cool breeze over a willow grove—surely a home is not made up of four concrete walls. A great saint had rightly said, 'Sacrifice a thousand houses for home.' At such times, a pain surfaces, a sting somewhere deep inside, a pinch of salt on a fresh wound.

A lost home is a lost life. A cruel joke! An existence of torture! A widow in prime youth! A separated lover! The pain of migration is a play of agony. Prophets have felt it with great sensitivity and with remarkable intensity. We are mere mortals.

I remembered the news item I had read that afternoon. All the words were clear in my memory.

'The Government of free Uzbekistan has announced that the year shall be suitably celebrated as the 66th anniversary of the great Amir Taimur. The nation will pay befitting homage to this great national hero that he so rightly deserves. The Government has further warned the public in general that anyone who may in foolishness call the Great Victor and unparalleled brave warrior Amir Taimur as Taimur Lang will be punished under the law and his tongue pulled out from the root...'

I laughed and laughed.

'What is the matter? What are you laughing at?' asked the shadow. I gave it a sharp look and said, 'You are right, I am in a fix, but that does not mean that I shall not be in a position to...'

The shadow grinned. I continued.

'Look, are you prepared to listen? Are you prepared to face the truth? If yes, then listen! Taimur was lame...only one leg... yes, he had only one leg...that's why he is known in history as Taimur Lang.'

'Oh! So this is the story...!'

My shadow was not prepared for this shock. Now it spoke with more maturity.

'Surely it is not civilised to call such a great hero Taimur Lang. It is very unfair...'

'I never said it is,' I shot back.

'Then?' the shadow retorted.

'Civilised people may not mention the name Taimur Lang,' I said angrily, 'but that does not mean Taimur wasn't lame.'

My shadow felt ashamed. It slinked away and almost disappeared. For long it could not speak. But I knew this was my own shadow. In the days of adversity my shadow had given me good company. When all was lost—mutual trust, love, affection, brotherhood, relationships—everything, and man was sectioned into fragments of hate—my shadow had not cared to leave me alone for a second. And now, when the fire in me is already doused and my days numbered, I will not part with it under any circumstances.

'You should understand the latent meaning of words,' I said, 'It is no use to cling to me and disturb me any time you like.'

My shadow looked into my eyes like a bull. I said, 'Why do you think that this story has ended at just this point?'

'Yes, it has. Maybe, the news has ended,' the shadow said reluctantly.

'Maybe the news,' I said, 'but not the story. The story has expanded. Many more angles, various other hues, other unknown dimensions of the story are now clear.'

'What do you mean?' the puzzled shadow asked.

'It is only after you come across a story,' said I, 'that the events and circumstances start unfolding. There is a process. Shadows have a bad habit of just aimlessly following others. I sometimes think your own shadow might be spying on those whom you follow. A trained agent of the enemy! Maybe it is working as a witness to many things that happen to us. Who knows! And as you know a man lives a life of struggle, and has his own share of sufferings and torture.'

The shadow was silenced. The doors of my consciousness opened wide. The wings of my mind fluttered. I said, 'Keep quiet and listen. You have no business to just follow me and unnecessarily blow the dust off the roads.'

'Then, say something,' said the shadow.

'What shall I say?'

'All that I do not know! But I wish to know everything. See, I have sealed my lips!'

I was forced to tell him everything right from the beginning. I said, 'Amir Taimur and Amir-e-Kabir Hazrat Amir Mir Sayed Ali Hamadani alias Shah-e-Hamadan were contemporaries. Both were from Persia, the most famous and civilized country in Central Asia. For twenty-one years, Amir Kabir travelled through various countries and during his travels he met the greatest of intellectuals, saints, and scholars of that age. He returned to his country in 1370 AD. At that time, Persia was in political turmoil; the social conditions had deteriorated. King Amir Taimur was at the peak of his glory. He terrorised people. He had become a law unto himself. He handed down his own brand of justice and targeted Sayeeds, the direct descendants of the Prophet of Islam, in particular. He hated them because he considered them his potential enemies. Consequently, many Sayeeds decided to migrate to safer places. A huge population of Sayeeds left Persia and travelled long and difficult distances to other neighbouring cities. Amir Kabir was sad. In utter disgust he left his country in 1372 AD along with 700 chosen disciples and travelled all the way to the beautiful valley of Kashmir.'

My shadow was listening to me with rapt attention and then suddenly asked, 'Who ruled Kashmir then?'

'At the time when Amir Kabir reached Kashmir,' I said, 'Sultan Shahab-ud-din Shahmiri was the ruler of Kashmir. He was not in Kashmir at that time. He was on a military expedition. His son Qutub-ud-Din was looking after the Kingdom, and he welcomed and received the Shah-e-Hamadan with fanfare.'

'What happened then?'

'This time Shah-e-Hamadan stayed in Kashmir only for six months. He left and came back after seven years. He stayed for two years and six months. The third time he came back to Kashmir in 1382 AD. He went away after staying in the valley for a brief period. He fell sick and then passed away in 1384 AD. His body was sent to Khatalaan where he was buried.'

My shadow froze again.

I discontinued the story. The landlord's warning of vacating the house rang again in my ears. But I could still say, 'This is a fact that Amir Kabir, and, later his son Hazrat Mir Hamad Hamadani deeply influenced and left indelible marks on the later history and culture of Kashmir.'

'They are clear and known, transparent and real,' my shadow agreed with me.

'Excellent!' I said, 'What fabulous demonstration of clear understanding!'

The landlord's house-vacating bell rang again. I felt a great fall. A fall from great heights!

'Oh, my God,' I cried, 'Do something for me. I have very little dignity left. Please, please, save it for the sake of my children. Something must be done today. If I am not able to settle my house problem today, I won't have a face to show my wife and children.'

I felt ashamed of myself. I felt naked, degraded, luckless, and wretched. What the hell was I doing? Asking for help? 'Asking' and 'demanding' help, attention. I have never prayed to God. Pity! I felt small. A strange pain emerged, a cancerous pain. The last stage was extremely unbearable. My body burned. Who would understand my pain? Who would feel the way I feel? I have a heart made of glass. There is a crack across it. Difficult for me to run with a broken glass-heart in my body!

Perhaps my shadow understood my pain. It has always been my companion—a long shadow, a short shadow, a shrunk shadow. Now I wept while I wanted to laugh partly at it and partly at myself. However, a question gnawed inside me. Had not Amir Kabir Mir Sayed Ali Hamadani been forced to migrate due to Amir Taimur and come to Kashmir, would the political and social conditions be as they are now?

I was meditating on this issue. The shadow asked, 'Should we Kashmiris call Taimur "Amir Taimur" or "Taimur Lang"?'

I could say nothing. My tongue was paralysed. I froze. My shadow clung to me.

(Translated from Kashmiri by C L Hakhoo)

The city of pain

Khema Kaul

SEVEN months after their exodus, Sudha's brother, putting his life at risk, goes to Srinagar and hires a truck. He seeks help from his very trustworthy Muslim friends, who initially are scared to lend a hand. However, they collect some necessary belongings and dump them into a truck.

His narration to his sister Sudha:

I recited the Indrakhi mantra. I forcibly tried to concentrate on the image of Lord Hanuman. Like a lunatic, I retrieved my own belongings as if I was on a looting spree. I handed the loose bundles to my friends with directions to deposit them in the truck. Majeed understood my predicament and tried to pacify me by saying, 'Kaka Ji, don't be afraid. Be courageous. The Prophet will save you and help you.'

Oh, my sister, even during this turmoil there were some souls around who hadn't become scoundrels. They were, indeed, in a minority. Then Hutchkukli came and said, 'Kaka, my son, give this gas cylinder to me.' I was taken aback. In spite of being so wealthy, she wanted to loot me. A mean bitch! May God crush such selfish looters!

You remember her brother-in-law who lives in House Number 80. He came and begged, 'Oh, this beautiful clock of yours is so exquisite. Will you please give it to me?' I remained mum. I was reconciled to the truth that I had lost all my rights. I was dismayed but I kept my cool. He noticed my silence and said immediately, 'Oh, I will give you some money. How much do you want for it?' I wanted to kill that beast, that wild animal. Was I there to auction my household goods? This bastard had come to collect his share of spoils. That whore Hutchkukli came first. They say it is against her Islamic faith. But her greed gives it religious sanction. Oh my God, save us from such people. Sometimes I ponder over it. Is it a fact that we lived with these people for so long? How? It is unbelievable. Yes, we had certain weaknesses. But who is without defects? I assure you we are real humans…humans of the first order. But they…?

SUDHA'S brother had gone to Lucknow that day to narrate his tale. He had narrated all this to Butni, his mother, as well. She had recoiled. She thought the house belonged to her. She considered herself lucky because her son had returned safe from Kashmir which had been turned into hell. She retained her courage to hear the tale. She repeatedly asked, 'Did you shut the doors and windows of our house properly? Did you lock the rooms properly? Did you secure the locks after you turned the keys? Did you lock all other doors? Did you lock the main gate?'

Irritated, he shouted, 'Yes, mother, yes.' He thought mother did not understand that a lock was useless. That all locks were useless. The circumstances were so terrifying that human values had come to naught. The loot and plunder was not done by the Mujahids but by the neighbours with whom there was love and camaraderie. He could not tell his mother all this. But he narrated everything to Sudha. I said to that beast, the brother-in-law of Hutchkukli, 'How can I fix a price tag for this clock? This is no time to do that. I am not here to sell things. You don't realise what turmoil I am in at this hour. You like the clock. You keep it. Even otherwise, I don't have a wall to hang this clock on. I live in a tattered tent. By all means keep this clock. Please treat it as your own possession.'

I still fail to understand whether I was laughing at my own predicament or ironically castigating that beast. I wanted to renounce everything.

And then? Sudha asked with bated breath.

The man triumphantly accepted it. There was a cruel sneer on his face.

And the gas cylinder? Oh Lord!

I am sure God was my helper. He put words into my mouth and solved the problem. I said to Hutchkukli: 'I have no objection in giving you the gas cylinder. There is no difference between you and us. Is there any difference between you and my mother? But come once and see for yourself how your own children are suffering there in the camps and how the food is cooked. My wife burns both her hands daily. Only then is the food cooked. Seeing the condition we are in, I am sure, Boba, you will present your own gas cylinder to me and say, "Take it, my son. Take any other thing that you require. Take this thing also." Believe me, we do not have anything there.'

'Oh, let it be. Take it,' the greedy woman said. But don't think that she took pity on us. She cared a tuppence. She thought, as an item of spoils, the gas cylinder belonged to her.

I remained mum during the loading of whatever I could take. Who could have believed that I would reach Lucknow and meet you? Here are the two sarees which you love and which your Prabhu Ji had bought for you. Then Hutchkukli's gaze fell on that extremely beautiful Japanese toy dog. There was a golden chain around its neck which she mistook for real gold.

Hearing this, Sudha was reminded of Pakistani Kabailis—raiders who invaded Kashmir in 1947—who mistook brass for gold because they had no knowledge of gold.

You know, Sudha, the greedy woman had heard that the toy had been imported from Japan. So she believed that the chain was made of real gold. She clung to the toy and implored, 'Kaka, give it to me, please.' At that time it was Goddess Sharika who made me say 'Yes, yes. Please take it. I am not worthy of possessing it. It has a gold chain around its neck. It will suit you better. Please, take it.'

'Allah…Swear, the chain is made of gold?'

'Sure, yes. Take the chain too. It doesn't matter.'

And then, Sudha, the greedy woman started to help me. She collected all the clothes that you had washed that day and bundled them. She wanted me to run away from my own home immediately. She was at peace with herself because of the chain, and she wanted to maintain that peace.

Jalboba…?

I didn't see her. But I heard that she was weeping because a house in front of her had fallen apart and was being looted. She was a passive spectator. Such neighbours could do nothing. 'Is this Islam?' she thought.

Hunh, Sudha muttered.

O yes, her son came to bid me farewell. The children also came. The women emerged with their eyes wet. All of them blessed me profusely. Jalboba's son said that his mother was reluctant to come out because she could not bear the sight. She prayed to God that the entire Hindu populace should soon return to their homes and hearths. 'The entire street shall have to face the retribution some day,' the old woman said.

Sudha was surprised. This is unbelievable, she said.

Yes, sister… But when I left in the truck, I cried. I was waving. People thought that I was waving to them whereas I was waving at my deserted lifeless house. Nobody knew whether I would ever return. I got the impression that you were still in the house and some sort of madness had made me run away after looting my own house. And you know, when I found myself in Jammu along with the belongings, I thought the whole thing was a dream. Your Bhabhi was in shock. There was no way to phone her. I could not call her during my journey. I was in for more trouble in Jammu. I faced it bravely because I was still alive after the ordeal. I learnt that in my absence my family had been shifted to another camp. After a long search, I found their tent. The truck driver was a noble man. He helped me a lot. If there were no tents, where would we have gone?

(Translated from Hindi by P L Waguzari)

Wedding album

Kishni Pandita

THE taxi stopped in front of the gate of a large house. A woman and her daughter got off the taxi. The woman, beautiful and elegant, was in her early forties. Her daughter was equally beautiful. The woman's gaze was uncertain. She was unsure about the surroundings. She surveyed the place. It had changed. Some of the houses looked different. Some of the old structures had caved in and new houses had been built. She was disappointed. Is it the same neighbourhood where I grew up? I don't know. I feel like a stranger, as if I don't belong here.

The lane was deserted. This was the same lane where she had raced on her bicycle, sometimes alone, and sometimes with her friends. Then she remembered a bow-legged young man. He literally stood on the pedals and rode his bicycle. People would make fun of him and call him 'zero legged'. One day, when some people had chased him he got very angry and shouted at them. She had seen her brothers chasing him too, chanting, 'zero legged, zero legged.' After that, the man was never seen there.

'Mama, you seem lost.'

'Oh! I went down the memory lane. I was reminded of my childhood. We had such wonderful experiences as children. But I am sorry that the same cannot be said about your childhood,' she said with moist eyes.

'But that was not your fault, Mama. You tried your best under the circumstances. I have no regrets, but growing up here with my cousins would have been a different kind of experience,' the daughter said.

'I don't know whose fault it was. Perhaps the Gods were angry with us. That's why they punished us by throwing us out.'

She turned and looked in the opposite direction. There was no one around. She wondered whether the milk shop at the end of the lane was still there. The thought of Saunder Goori bai, the woman who sold milk and curd brought a smile to her face. Saunder was fair complexioned with deep blue eyes. Her husband was a hunchback. Even as a child she had wondered how she had married him. Whenever she went to buy curd from the shop, Saunder would always place a spoonful of it on her palm. She would then lick if off her palm slowly. Then she would wipe her mouth on the hem of her frock.

Last time, when she had gone to see her mother during the summer holidays she had confessed to her that she continued to accept some extra curd from Saunder in spite of her orders not to take anything from anyone. Her mother had smiled and told her that she knew everything. 'There would always be tell-tale marks on your mouth. But I decided to ignore them. After all, you were only a child.'

So much for my best kept secret, she thought. But then mother had been too smart to be duped. Nothing escaped her. She wasn't the same person she had been. Migration, father's death and the separation from her loved ones had made her old and grey.

'I am not sure about this door because it looks different,' she said to her daughter, pointing her finger towards the direction of a house. 'You had always wanted to see our house. This should be it but I am a little uncertain because so much has changed now.'

She lifted the latch somewhat hesitantly. To her surprise, the huge door swung open with a jarring sound. She stepped inside gingerly and her daughter followed. The poplar trees on the path leading to the house had been cut. Only the stumps were left, the, sad reminders of the tall and elegant trees. For years they had been the sentinels guarding the house. Those poplars had been the landmarks. The courtyard was full of tall grass. It resembled a jungle. It was difficult to imagine that there used to be a lush green vegetable garden full of brinjals, chillies, cucumbers and other vegetables.

The house stood mute and still. The broken windowpanes, the shut windows and doors told a tale of their own. The house looked sad, desolate, forsaken and forlorn. It broke her heart to see such desolation around the house she was born and brought up in. The house was missing its occupants. Once it had been a beehive of activity, especially in the mornings when everyone got together to begin the day. There would be singing and screaming. Mother would have a tough time meeting everyone's demands. And now the same mother was in a different corner of the country, as desolate and forlorn as the house itself.

A tear trickled down her cheek. Her vision blurred. Old memories came alive. She saw her elder sister holding her hand to escort her to school. She saw her other sister combing her hair and putting her school satchel on her shoulders. Her mother putting her tiffin box in her satchel, planting a kiss on her cheek and reminding her to eat food on time; her brother taking her for a ride on the bicycle and her pigtails flying in the air. Once their father had scolded both of them for being reckless. 'What if your sister gets hurt? Why can't you go a little slow? What is the big hurry?' he had said. 'Don't worry, Father, nothing bad will happen. See how her cheeks are glowing and how happy she looks,' brother had said.

One more tear trickled down. Some more images from her childhood flashed before her. Her brothers were playing cricket. She and her sisters were sitting on the steps giving head massages to each other and the game was in full swing. The ball hit the wicket and there was a loud uproar. 'Howzaaat!' She shouted loudly, 'fowzaat…fowzaat.'

'What happened, Mama? And what is fowzaat?' A smile appeared on her face.

'When I was your age, I didn't know what it was they shouted when someone got out. I thought they said fowzaat. They would laugh. I didn't know why they laughed. Later, I realised that they made fun of me. I will never forget the laughter of my friends when we played Seven Stones. We ran into other houses, banged doors and jumped fences. Sometimes we got a scolding but we were carefree.'

'Thank God your memories have brought a smile on your face. You looked miserable a moment ago. Where are the pomegranate trees that you talked about?

'I can't see them. Perhaps they met the same fate as the poplars. But why would someone chop off the trees?'

'And where is the well? I would like to see it,' my daughter said.

'It is over there but with this wild grass it is not possible to see it. I feel scared walking through the grass. You really don't know what insects are hiding in it. Let us forget about it.'

She shivered. She looked around with dismay. It was a bleak sight. 'This is the same compound where we crafted snowmen in the winters. Our hands would go numb with cold but it was so much fun. How we used to laugh and roll in the snow. The snowmen had charcoal eyes, crescent-shaped mouths and cigarettes dangling off their lips. They wore battered caps and old coats. There would also be snow fights amongst us. We threw snowballs at each other. Because I was the youngest, I was spared.'

Suddenly she realised that they had been there for quite some time. Somebody might accuse them of trespassing. 'Let us go to the house we have come for. I am feeling a bit nervous. I don't know how the current occupants are going to react. Just hope they are good people and don't mind our visit.'

They opened the main gate and climbed the steps of the verandah. The door inside was closed. The knocked for some time but nobody came out. She tried once again and finally they heard footsteps.

'Sorry, I was in the bathroom,' a woman said. She wore a velvet *pheran* with exquisite zari embroidery. She was beautiful. 'Sorry, I am not able to recognise you,' she said.

'No, you wouldn't. My name is Archana Bhan, and this is my daughter, Vaibhavi. This house was ours…I mean, we used to live here…'

'Oh is that so? I am Asmat. Please come in,' said the woman.

They went inside.

'This house is unrecognisable. This is not how we had left it,' Archana said marvelling at the decor of the house.

'When we purchased the house, it was in a rundown condition because it had been lying vacant for a long time. It needed overhauling. Let us have some tea. We can talk and then I will show you the rest of the house,' Asmat said.

'Please don't bother. We don't wish to inconvenience you. If you don't mind we will take a look around and leave,' Archana said.

'Please don't say that. I am so happy to see you. This is your house and you have every right to see it. By the way, Archana, you have changed a lot.'

'Not only changed but aged, too. But how do you know that?' Archana was surprised at Asmat's remark.

'Some years ago, I found a photograph of a young girl,' said Asmat. 'The name Archana was written on the back of the photo. I have the photograph. I wondered where the girl was. I am a little sentimental you see. I will make some tea and then you can tell me everything about yourself.'

Strange thoughts clouded Archana's mind. 'Tell me, Archana, how is it that you did not take anything with you when you left your house and this place?' Asmat asked.

'I didn't leave with the intention of not returning. I had gone to Chandigarh for treatment. Vaibhavi was only one and a half months old when I developed a gynaecological problem. There were no good doctors here. The three of us left with only one suitcase thinking that we would be back in two weeks. The truth is that we were not allowed to enter the hospital here in Srinagar. They said that the hospital was not meant for Pandits. My parents and my in-laws had to beg the authorities to let us in. That was also one of the reasons that we decided to go to Chandigarh for my treatment.'

'How inhuman!'

'When we returned to Jammu after my treatment we found that the place was flooded with Pandits. You know what had happened. Pandits had been threatened, terrorised and even killed in Kashmir. They had no choice but to leave. We were terrified. There was no place to stay and we had nothing with us. My in-laws who were in Srinagar were helpless. They advised us not to return home because militants were targeting Pandits. We had not left with the intention of leaving our home forever but… This girl, my daughter, has faced a lot of difficulties. Even if she lives in a palace and eats off a golden plate, I will not be satisfied because it is difficult to forget what we went through and endured. The wounds may have healed with the passage of time but the scars won't go away. I still get nightmares and there are things which still haunt me after all these years.' Archana broke down.

'It is all right, Mama. All of that darkness has dispelled now. You weren't at fault,' Vaibhavi said comforting her.

'It wasn't my fault but it wasn't yours either. Why did you have to face horrible conditions? It was torturous and agonising. We were helpless. We were forced to live in pathetic conditions. We had to scrounge for basic necessities. It was so embarrassing to ask others for help. There was no bed, no bedding, just the bare floor, that too not our own but somebody else's.' Archana wiped her tears. 'All of us went through the same hell. You couldn't expect much help from anyone. But there were people who did whatever they could under the circumstances and I will be eternally grateful to them. Doing small things made a big difference. It reminded us that there were still people who believed in benevolence and valued humanity. Many families were staying together. Most of us were in a state of shock. Many of us believed that we would go back to the comfort of our homes. But there was no sign of normalcy in Srinagar. In fact, the conditions kept deteriorating. You were our princess. And we couldn't give you the comfort you deserved. We had no money to bear the expenses. We had to start from scratch. All our belongings were here. And we were so far away, unable to return,' Archana said to Vaibhavi.

'I am so sorry about everything that happened to you,' said Asmat. 'Many of us did not like the way the situation unfolded. For generations we had stayed together peacefully. You do believe that all of us didn't approve of the things that took place here those days.'

'Of course we believe that. I still have many Muslim friends who are closer to me than my own people. We shouldn't generalise and paint everyone with the same brush,' Archana said, holding Asmat's hands.

'Thank you for understanding! During the peak of militancy, sanity, logic and reason vanished. Only chaos prevailed. The youth had been fed on false rumours. So much wrong information, aggression and hatred had been pumped into them that they had gone berserk. Liberal supply of weapons made them trigger-happy. All the anger against the central government and corrupt politicians was directed against innocent people. They not only killed Pandits but Muslims, too, who did not support them in their so-called jihad. No religion teaches violence but who will make them understand. All sorts of anti-social elements joined them including some from across the border,' Asmat said.

'I know that whenever there was communal violence in other parts of the country Kashmir had always remained untouched. Even Gandhi, during the communal frenzy at the time of partition, said that he saw a ray of hope in Kashmir. Murders and killings were unheard of here. Once our father told us about an incident that took place in his childhood. He must have been about nine or ten years old. There was communal tension in the city. Our ancestral home was in the old city. Ours was the only Pandit household. We were surrounded by Muslims but we shared very good relations with them. During the tension, one elderly man who was my grandfather's friend came to him and told him that there was a rumour that they might be attacked and the idols of their Gods placed in their house would be desecrated. He wanted him to shift the idols to his house. My father was made to do the job. He returned home unharmed, despite the threats. That was the trust and concern that we had for one another. We never allowed our faiths to come in the way of our friendships,' Archana said.

'That's right. Let's go and see the rest of your house.' Asmat took them around the house. There were chandeliers in all rooms.

'You should call it the Chandelier House,' said Archana. Vaibhavi was dazzled by all the glitter of the chandeliers.

'And this is your bedroom,' Asmat said as she led them inside. Archana didn't know how to respond. How many times had she dreamt of her room! This was the room she had entered as a bride years ago. She had started her new life here. She had shared sweet moments with her husband. She had her own cupboard, her own bed. She cried and cried. Asmat had a difficult time controlling her. Vaibhavi went to the window. 'Mama, we can see your ancestral house from here,' she said.

'Yes, I know. This is the window from where your father used to follow me with his gaze,' she said smiling. With a twinkle in his eyes he would wait for me to look back and give him a smile. I would watch him from the window of my house,' she said pointing towards the window of a house nearby.

'Poor Papa!' Vaibhavi said.

'Archana, this house is as much yours as it is mine,' Asmat said. Please bring your whole family here. I will keep your room ready for you? Archana was overwhelmed. 'And I have something for you. Let me get it.'

'Please don't do this. You have been so nice, that's good enough. No gifts please,' Archana said.

'First you should see what I have for you and then you must decide whether you would like to take it or not.'

Asmat opened an almirah and took out an album.

'Oh, my God!' Archana said in excitement and shock. 'This is my wedding album! I had thought I had lost it. I just can't believe that I am holding it in my hands after all these years,' she said looking fondly at her album. 'Thank you so much, Asmat. I don't have the words to describe how I am feeling right now. Thank you for not throwing it away.'

'When we bought the house, it was almost vacant, bereft of any possessions. But in a pile of rubble I came upon this album. I cleaned it and kept it safely, thinking that perhaps someday you would come looking for it,' Asmat said.

Archana was speechless. Tears flowed down her cheeks as she flipped through the pages of the album and saw photos of herself as a bride.

The last cry

Shilpa Raina

June 30
1990
8 am

AN unusual activity at home has stirred up the morning. Mother's eyes are battling against tiredness. The packed belongings and household items strewn across the rooms in our four-storeyed house have been a witness to the long, sleepless night we have endured.

Yet, there is a strong sense of unpreparedness. The look on the faces of mother and father is unsure. But they know they must remain watchful. The decision to leave home has been debated inside candle-lit rooms and in hushed tones behind carefully drawn curtains to ensure that whispers rolling out of the trembling lips don't reach the outside world. There were days when the thought of leaving home was contemplated several times, much against the wishes of my grandfather. But no one ever arrived at any conclusion, as if no one wanted to be blamed for 'giving in'. During the day, mother and father pretend to be fearless, but every night when loud and terrifying voices blaring from the loudspeakers of a mosque are heard, fear grips their hearts; hearts talk to hearts, eyes to eyes, betraying agony and hopelessness. The voices are threatening. Are 'they' coming for us? Are we the 'targets'?

After all, the 'story' they have heard during the preceding months has now started playing out in front of their eyes. The story of our eviction from our homes! 'You will have to leave this place,' we had been told.

It isn't easy to interpret or decipher the changes that are taking place in our locality. Who would have imagined that we would be caught in a tornado of fear and violence? The image of blood in the street flashes and inflicts pain. The image of being dragged and pulled, beaten and threatened! Our lives are at stake. Our identity, too! This is where the unpreparedness stems, the uncertainty looming over us and the other households. Like the brave hearts reluctant to leave, my family too is determined not to give up the fight. No, we won't leave. We won't give up. Not so easily. We are among the last few families trying to linger on by living an invisible life in our own neighbourhood, like fugitives in hiding to be precise. Father is trying hard not to feel intimidated by the threats he has been receiving at regular intervals from the masked men who come knocking on our door and hand over warning letters. 'Leave, or be ready for the consequences,' say the letters. He has been ignoring the warnings. Until now he has been praying and hoping for the situation to change for the better.

But something changed his opinion last week. As a result, we are all set to leave home. Despite having an entire week to ourselves, the house is a chaotic mess; everyone is confused. The truck has arrived at our doorstep. It is going to take our belongings and us to Jammu. Everyone is nervous and anxious. What's going to happen now? What should be done? Mother and father have taken positions to assist each other in loading the household possessions on to the truck. Big and heavy things first. Small and lightweight things last.

'SHOULD we carry these jackets and woollens and blankets,' mother asks father.

'We won't need them in Jammu. It's hot as hell there, and hopefully, we will be back soon.'

'What if there is no coming back? What shall we do then? We should at least carry some woollens,' grandmother says, as if she knows what's going to happen in future.

'That won't happen. We will come back before summer. Who wants to get roasted in the terrible heat there?' grandfather interrupts. He's dejected. 'I know the weather there. I have experienced it. We won't survive the heat,' he warns, remembering his early years at Udhampur in the early 80s when he was on a teaching assignment there.

'We should carry only necessary things. We should travel light. We have to pack the belongings of others as well. Let's focus on things that are useful and absolutely vital,' father says.

'Does this mean there will be no room in the truck for my books?' grandfather whispers.

'What kind of illogical things you say sometimes?' grandmother blurts out infuriated. The look on her face betrays annoyance. 'I am amazed. Here we are trying to pack things that hold immense value and will be of use to us in an alien city, and you are still obsessed with your books.'

'This is why I have been telling you that I don't want to leave. But no one ever listens to me. Don't involve me in this talk. Take whatever you want,' grandfather says annoyingly and leaves the room abruptly.

GRANDFATHER'S world is centered solely on books—his priceless possessions. He has collected books for most of his life. Our house has many rooms and there are books in each of the rooms. In the top floor of the house, grandfather, whom we call Papa, has piled books upon books, magazines upon magazines, and papers upon papers. It's a wall of books around the reading space. A treasure trove for bookworms and research scholars! Papa is a scholar of repute. He holds two Master's degrees, one in Economics and one in Political Science. He has earned the reputation of being a reliable and diligent professor. Many of his students are Muslims. He's retired from the government college, but still teaches at a high school near Dal Gate. But for the past few days, he hasn't stepped out of the house. I feel someone in the neighbourhood is keeping an eye on me, he says to my father. He is suspicious. What he says resembles a movie scene in which a character fears being closely monitored in his own locality. Why would anyone keep an eye on him? After all, he is just a professor whose only interests in life are teaching and reading.

His unwillingness to leave has a lot to do with his obsessive attachment to the books in his library. The very idea of leaving home, his revered space, is agonising. He is content in the tiny world he has created for himself. The world of books and writings! Reading is what gives him strength and sustenance. Philosophy and history, economics and literature keep him occupied. His unwillingness to leave is making everyone at home worried. On June 23, Prithvi Nath Tikku, our neighbour, was killed by the militants right outside his home. His killing was a sign that no one from our community was safe.

At last, grandfather gives in to the mounting pressure. But he doesn't give up the hope to return. He doesn't want to come out of his room.

June 30 1990 7 am

GRANDMOTHER has taken charge of cooking, and mother has decided to help father in loading the luggage on to the truck. Papa has just come back from the ration depot after purchasing sugar. He wants to ensure we don't have to worry about food supplies.

The process of loading has commenced and there is synchronised action. A porter is helping father carry the luggage to the truck. Mother is supervising and keeping a close watch. Papa has decided to park himself near the truck to keep vigil and arrange the items properly.

The truck is parked inside the compound of our neighbour's house at the far end of the lane. My two-year-old brother and I are standing near the gate of our house to supervise the porter and to be at our father's beck and call, just in case he requires us to run any errands. My brother and I are unable to conceal our excitement. The prospect of meeting our cousins and other family members who are already in Jammu is the secret of our excitement.

'Both of you keep holding the fort here, and I will see you in some time,' Papa whispers to us as he walks away.

Everything is progressing fine. Moments pass. A faint shriek sends a shiver down our spines. We hear it again and this time it is loud. *Morhosa* (I am being killed). The ominous shriek is coming from the lane. I am petrified because I know something terrible has happened. My brother is ahead of me. We look into each other's eyes not knowing what has happened. The main gate of our house is wide open. We don't know what to do. Before we muster courage to inspect the surroundings, my father orders us to go inside and hide. He bolts the gate from outside and rushes out.

MY mother is anxious. Every now and then she asks me to look outside through a chink in the window of the main hall. See what's going on there, she says in a hushed tone, pointing towards the porch of our Muslim neighbour's house. The porch is framed in the window. An hour goes by. Father is yet to return. The ominous shriek still echoes. The shriek interrupts the luggage loading process. Half of our belongings are in the truck and the rest in the house. Mother has reasons to feel upset at the delay in our departure. Poor porter, she whispers, thinking that the dying shriek was his.

Father is nowhere to be seen. 'How can he be so careless and forgetful,' mother fumes. 'He always behaves like this…' We are in a huddle in the hall, waiting for father to return. Until now, the hall has always been a witness to good and happy times. This is where everyone would meet up after a day's work to sit together and talk. This hall has never seen gloom like the one it is wrapped in right now. It has seen happier days.

The hall is now witnessing a sinister silence and eeriness that came with the departure of my uncles and their families. One by one they all left. From twelve, we are now reduced to six. And today, if all goes as planned, it is going to be our last day in the house.

A few steps away from our neighbour's house, where my brother and I were standing a while ago, is a pool of blood. The blood of the porter, believes my mother. She peeks out of the window, hoping to catch a glimpse of my father. The truck is gone, too. There's no sign of it. Has Papa already left? Has he left us behind? Or is this a joke? What's going on?

Mother says a silent prayer for the poor porter.

Moments pass in trepidation.

MOTHER'S gaze is fixed on the clock. She stares at me intermittently. As a nine-year-old caught in an uncertain situation I am on the verge of breaking down. I hear Mother say, 'Can you please go to the window and call your father and ask him to hurry up if at all he responds to your call.' I pretend not to listen and continue playing with a furry rabbit.

She gets up and looks out of the window. She can only see a shadow of my father who is surrounded by a posse of policemen. Grandmother is quiet. She knows her son is always forthcoming when it comes to helping others. My brother has fallen asleep, and the awkward silence continues to reign.

VOICES…

'I saw them. They were two young boys. I couldn't see their faces because their backs were towards me. I heard a loud cry. I was near the truck, and by the time I reached the spot, they had already killed him,' a man says to the policemen. He pauses and begins again. 'I immediately rushed to the spot and brought him here. I poured some water into his mouth, but he was dead by then.'

'He has been shot twice,' the policeman says. 'One bullet in the chest and another in the neck. We will have to take the body for the post-mortem.'

In our family, my father is the one entrusted with the responsibility of taking care of everyone. Having sensed trouble, he had earlier asked his younger brothers to shift to Jammu for safety. For them it was easier. One was working for a bank, so getting a transfer was easy; the younger one had started his career.

It is his business that has kept Father glued to his house. He hasn't even made a profit yet. He, too, like many others, wasn't prepared for the uncertainty the future had in store. The thought of having to set up a business all over again in a new city was daunting.

With this gruesome incident, everything seems to have collapsed. We're faced with new worries.

ANOTHER hour has passed and father is still at the neighbour's house. Mother is exasperated by now. She has lost her patience. Traces of frustration are visible on her face, as the ticking clock signals an endless delay. Her questions are unanswered. Fear has invaded our hearts. Father's unwarranted presence in the neighbour's house and his continued participation in the interrogation of the porter's merciless killing is driving my mother insane. Doesn't he care for us? Mother wonders.

Suddenly, panic seizes her. Her throat becomes dry. Something is not right. She starts babbling.

'What if it wasn't the porter?'

She pauses. The look on her face is frightening.

'What if? No! It can't be true. This can't happen to us. But then, why is he still there? Is he…?'

Dreadful thoughts and visions cloud her mind.

Am I hallucinating?

She can't go out because the main gate is bolted from outside. But then she gets up hurriedly and rushes towards the window through which she had seen the pool of blood. I have been trying to read her face because suddenly she has become quieter, more contemplative, and her tired eyes show signs of fear.

I follow her. I'm curious to see the pool of blood. Mother is absent-minded and doesn't mind me following her. Oblivious to her fears, I look out of the window standing next to her. The lane is deserted. I look towards the far end of the lane. The image of the pool of blood sticks to me. I can't get rid of it.

We wait and wait. Just as I am about to go back into the room a man enters the lane. His face is familiar. He is from the neighbourhood. He comes close to the main gate of our house.

'Can you tell me what has happened there?' Mother asks.

The man looks puzzled. He looks at my mother in astonishment, and then says, 'You don't know? Professor Nila Kanth Raina has been killed.'

My heart stops.

The mirage

Monika Ajay Kaul

WHILE coming back from her school, Haerath was waiting for her four-year-old brother's school bus to arrive. The bus was late. Ten minutes… twenty minutes… an hour passed; but there was no sign of the bus. Haerath's anxiety was increasing. Her heart beat fast. Others waiting for the bus started praying for the safe arrival of the kids.

I hope everything is alright with the kids and nothing untoward has happened, Haerath thought. She kept her fingers crossed.

This wasn't the end of the woes for the parents. Suddenly, a panic-stricken mob from the opposite direction started running here and there. There was confusion and tension and chaos all around. Some people started pelting stones at an army bunker.

Everyone tried to run away from the stone-pelters. Haerath was to cross the bridge to reach home.

Meanwhile, the school bus arrived while everyone was confused about the next move. Haerath gathered herself together in spite of the fear that gripped her. She held her brother's hand firmly as he got off the bus.

How to reach home? she wondered.

Hesitantly, yet bravely, she put her foot forward. She had hardly walked a few paces when a hand from behind stopped her.

'O, Azhar Bhaijaan! I am going home. But…' Haerath said nervously.

'I know. Come with me. Hurry up! We don't have much time,' he said. He was ill-at-ease.

'No, I can't. Jiji is waiting for me. I've to reach home and I'm late. I cannot go anywhere else,' said Haerath.

Before she could resist, the boy gripped her arm and hauled her towards the bank of the Jhelum. The bridge that they were to cross could be seen from the bank. But her gaze was stuck at the maddening crowd—stone pelters and protestors who were the cause of the ruckus. She trembled at the sight. Her grip over her little brother's tiny arm stood firm. The little boy was unaware of the reasons behind the commotion that was taking place. Haerath prayed for the ordeal to end.

Azhar Bhaijaan was her cousin's childhood friend. Haerath knew him well. So she let her apprehensions go. She watched him talk to a boatman. She watched them in bewilderment. Her heart was beating fast and her legs were trembling.

'Come, come. Hurry up. We must cross over to the other side,' Azhar said authoritatively.

Haerath's trepidation was still alive.

She resisted, 'No, I cannot go like this. Call someone from my home.'

The gush of the waters of Jhelum was scary.

Azhar understood Haerath's anxiety. He once again held her arm and made her sit in the boat. He presented himself as a saviour. Apprehensions gripped Haerath. The boat carrying the occupants wobbled.

'Sit down and stop worrying. You're safe. We are going home.'

Azhar took a pack of Poppins out of his pocket and handed it over to the little boy. It held his attention for a while.

Haerath was restless and in a dilemma. Would mom have reached home by now? Is she okay? Uncertainty and doubt plagued her.

The boat was sailing against the current which made it difficult for it to ply. Azhar Bhaijaan helped the boatman pull on the oars with more force. Eventually, Haerath saw familiar houses. She saw the temple where she went on the weekends with her grandmother, Jiji.

Across the road was her home. Imagining it at that moment wasn't easy.

HAERATH was a dewy-eyed girl. Her sparkling hazel eyes and the colour of hair were bewitching. Her innocence and beauty made the boys stammer.

Haerath's usual wake-up time was a quarter-to-seven. Hastily she would climb down the stairs from her room on the first floor towards Jiji's room and jump into the warmth of her granny's bed. Cuddling her in bed every morning was a custom followed without fail.

'Jiji, please shift a little. I can't fit in!' she would say.

'Oh Haerath, it's getting late now. I need to get up,' Jiji would reply.

'Just some more time, Jiji.'

Jiji would pamper Haerath by stroking her silky hair till she fell asleep. Haerath couldn't go to bed unless her grandma stroked and patted her. Jiji was an ace at washing utensils, performing puja, cooking delicacies and narrating tales. Her room had a mystic aura and smelt of dried flowers. An aroma of joss sticks wafted in her room all the time. On the weekends, Haerath accompanied her granny to the temple on the bank of Jhelum. The place was like a beautiful, mesmerising painting. Haerath used to draw and paint beautiful landscapes on her drawing sheets.

By and by, Haerath too understood that something wasn't right in Kashmir. One day, a terrible occurrence shook her. One fateful morning in September 1989, a family friend, returning after paying a visit to their place was shot near their lane. He had been a noted lawyer, social and political activist of Kashmir. But Haerath knew him as a dear uncle and a good human being.

'Maeji…!' (Mother) the man used to shout from the gate till he would reach the doorway.

The refrain—I'm here, Mother—was followed by amicable conversations with the family members, especially Haerath's grandmother, Jiji. Every week, he would visit their home and pamper granny like his own mother. That day too, as usual, he had a cup of tea and left. Barely five minutes had passed when gunshots were heard. What followed was chaos in the lane and adjacent areas. It shattered Jiji.

Time rolled by amidst confusion and chaos. Life started rolling down on a road to nowhere. A dead-end was about to approach. Each passing day, the news of killings, kidnappings, violence and communal unrest came. The deadly creeper spread its poisonous branches in the vale of the sages.

The day of terror supervened. Aghast and disheartened, people were clueless. An uncertain future awaited them. Everyone was anguished. Everything seemed unsettling. The beautiful idyllic winter of Kashmir appeared sombre and funerary.

Then one pensive night, loud and vengeful announcements started echoing in the valley. They reverberated in all directions.

'What's this? What is going on? Who is shouting?' Haerath's awkward questions didn't stop while everyone was having dinner.

Jiji and Haerath's mother had no clue. Haerath's father was posted in a different city. Lack of electricity and connectivity made it unnerving. The board examinations were cancelled. Absence of any clarity of the present and future happenings made it worse.

As the hush-hush talk was going on between the two elderly women, deep within Haerath an inconclusive unrest and turmoil took birth.

Outside, a deadly creeper hungry for human flesh was crouching towards the house. Time was progressing ahead in uncertainty and disquietude. Everything appeared cold and forbidding. An aura of unfriendliness was taking over. Never ever had the people experienced such fear.

The cataclysmic night arrived, the night which was as dark as a black hole. It pushed the family to places where there was no light, only darkness.

There was an abrupt knock at the door. Everyone shuddered. The women were startled. 'Papa...! I'm sure, it's a surprise visit!' was Haerath's instant cry.

A smile flickered on her brother's innocent face. Haerath stood up in excitement to open the door after another knock.

'Sit down, Haerath,' her mother said. She stood up and through a chink in the window peeped like a thief. Exchanging glances with Jiji, she confirmed, 'Haej Sahib.'

'Let me open the door. We need not worry.' Jiji gave an intrepid reply and dashed to open the door.

Their neighbour stood on the other side of the massive door. After exchanging the customary greetings, the uninvited guest entered the foyer along with his wife. They started talking to the women of the house in hushed tones.

'You must leave tomorrow. Other Pandits from the neighbourhood are leaving too, and we shall see you soon, *Inshah Allah*.'

A few more shocking utterances tailed the conversation. The couple left hurriedly as if they were afraid of something.

After exchanging a few words the family started preparing. They decided to leave the next morning.

'But Mom…we are supposed to leave next week. Our tickets are booked for Delhi. Papa is supposed to join us there. Why are we leaving now in a hurry?' Haerath asked question after question. There was annoyance on her face.

'Go to your room with your brother, Haerath. We will talk in the morning,' her mother said faking a smile.

Next morning, Haerath woke up thinking that everything that she had seen and heard was a dream.

'Get up, sweetheart; get ready. And tell your brother to be ready quickly. We are leaving in an hour.'

The words shattered her.

'Mom, I haven't packed my stuff, my books and other things. What about the new shoes and dresses that we bought for the marriage ceremony?' Haerath asked.

Her mom smiled a sheepish smile.

'I have packed the important stuff, you need not worry.' Within an hour, all of them were ready with two suitcases, one large bag and her father's briefcase with important documents in it. The things were kept in the courtyard. Jiji locked the beautifully carved door. They were about to leave their nest.

THE house had witnessed many beautiful seasons come and go. Haerath was in love with the house. Jiji had lived in it for her entire life. She was a teenager when she had arrived here as a bride. She had come with plenty of dreams. But those dreams were short-lived. Haerath's grandfather had died at an early age, leaving Jiji with two little children and a toddler. He had lost everything in his business.

A few neighbours were waiting outside. Haji Uncle, auntie and their daughter, with whom Haerath had shared her childhood dolls and teenage secrets, stood there biding them goodbye with heavy hearts.

'*Khuda-hafiz.* We will meet again, *Inshah Allah*,' were the last words.

A storm raged in their hearts. The dark Banihal Tunnel disjointed them from the avenues that led to their homes.

Haerath cried.

MONTHS earlier, Haerath had entered the attic on the fourth floor of the house and discovered a treasure. The attic was dusty. Her curiosity had compelled her to explore the nooks and corners. She had chanced upon a pile of books. 'Mom, Mom! You need to take a look at this. Please come. Hurry up,' Haerath had said excitedly.

'What is it, Haerath? What have you seen? What happened?'

'You need to come upstairs. I want to show you something.'

Haerath's mother had followed her to the attic.

'What do you want me to see?'

'Whose books are these? Why haven't you told me about these books? Can I take some of them to my room?'

'Hold on girl, take only a few. I don't want your room to be a mess.'

THEY reached the destination safe; it was a destination little known to them.

A terrible life was to commence for thousands of people… a new life, obscure and bleak. Days, months and years followed. A graceful community had now a new status to flaunt: 'Migrants', 'Refugees', and 'Displaced'. That was not enough. Some called them 'traitors'. It was a parting gift to them from the places they had left. Others called them 'cowards'.

The suffering was immense for the elderly. They started to perish one after another. The young struggled to get accustomed to living in hostile conditions in camps and tents. The toilets presented horrible scenes. There was no water. There were no trees. There was no electricity. Everyone saw things that didn't exist. 'Look, there is our home,' said one person who seemed to have lost his mind.

'Don't believe in the mirages,' said a doctor who came to treat patients in the camp. 'It is the heat which is causing them.'

Years passed. More mirages. More hallucinations. More haze. No hope.

One evening, a colleague of Haerath's father visited them. After a long conversation he slowly and hesitantly uttered the words: 'There was a fire in your locality. Your house was gutted in the fire.' Her father casually asked the guest, 'Can you do me a favour?'

'Yes, of course. Just tell me what to do,' was his reply.

'Jiji owes some money to a few people. Can you return them their dues?' Haerath's father mentioned the name of a local grocery owner and a milk woman of their locality.

'It will be done,' the guest said.

Haerath's father handed over some money to his colleague. The guest left. At dinner time, Jiji refused to eat anything.

'I am not hungry. I want to sleep,' was the reply. Looking at her daughter-in-law with a blank face she asked for a cup of Kehwa.

Jiji slept and never woke up.

She bid adieu to the mirage. The mirage of her lost home. She no longer carried any debts now. All Haerath could do was to kiss Jiji's cold cheeks and whisper in her ears: 'Home is wherever you are, Jiji. I'm sorry.'

Haerath would often tell her, 'I wish I could see you as a young girl.'

It was a difficult thing for Haerath to imagine her granny like that. The reason was that she had seen her benevolence and heard about her fighting spirit. But her grandmother had never spoken of her horrors.

As they took Jiji for the last rites, Haerath visualised the remnants of her home.

It used to be vibrant. It had been a haven of love and certainty, a place full of souvenirs and treasures. Now it was just a ruin. Haerath felt the heat of the bright flames on her face.

Somewhere in that rubble that once was 'Home', all of their possessions had turned into ash.

Haerath lived a quiet life thereafter, pinning her hope on the mirage that kept bringing her images of a lost home.

Avenged

Sushant Dhar

VIJAY and Rouf were childhood friends. They were the favourites of their school cricket team. Their roll numbers were 1 and 2. Their school was situated on the banks of Jhelum in Chattapura, a small idyllic village in South Kashmir. The lanes and houses nearby bore marks of the people who once thrived there. The two rivers feeding the valley converged behind the mountain facing the village.

Twenty-one years after the exodus of the Pandits from the Kashmir Valley, Asha murmured, 'When will this exile end? When will we go home? Lord, who will protect us? Where is our saviour? May God repay them for what they did to us!' She dreamt of Yarbal, the bank of Jhelum, and her elder son, Ramesh. Ramesh's ashes had been immersed in the Jhelum.

The day Asha left her house in Kashmir she had insisted on taking the newly born calf with her. But unsure of the calf's safety, she leaned towards her, kissed her head and handed her over to Rasool Khan. She said to him, 'Keep her safe, I will come back for her.' She begged him to feed the calf well. She gave him some money and left teary-eyed. The calf ran after Asha and even tried to climb on to the truck that was taking Asha's family away.

A few months later, when Asha heard that the calf had been slaughtered a week after they had fled, she was furious at Rasool Khan. She wept for the entire day.

THE narrator of this story died in exile in 1998. His name was Vyad Kak. He was a short story writer. He didn't marry. He had no family. He had lost his parents in the Pakistani tribal raid of 1947. It had caused him immense pain. He had lost his memory in exile. Vyad Kak had been close to Bishambar Nath's family. When he died, all the books kept in his room were distributed among camp children. I still possess an old Sanskrit edition of *Bhagvad Gita* that belonged to him. V.K 1934 is inscribed on the flyleaf of the book. I found his high school marksheet buried in the pages. It read:

University of Jammu & Kashmir
Vyad Kak
First Division
1950.

It was 9.30 by the clock. The tape recorder played an old song, *Yeh duniya agar mil bhi jaaye to kya hai*. Rani had slept early. Asha was cooking food. Bishambar Nath had gone to the nearby village for some work. Vijay and his elder brother Ramesh were playing cards. Ramesh stood up and looked through the window. A group of men were laughing outside. A shadow ran past the window. The laughter grew louder. Sounds of the stamping of boots were heard. The front door of the house opened with loud noise from the banging of the door. Several men wearing pherans entered the house. The faces of some of the intruders were covered. 'Where is Bishambar Nath? Where is that traitor? Where is that rascal?' The intruders shouted incessantly and furiously. Two of them sat by the windows wielding their guns. Vijay curled himself into a corner of the room. Ramesh trembled with fear. One of the intruders went straight to the kitchen. Asha shouted frantically, 'Who are you? Why are you here? What do you want? What wrong have we done? What are you going to do to us?' She ran from one room to the other making sure Vijay and Ramesh were not in sight. She saw Rani sleeping in the other room. She quickly bolted the door of the room.

The intruders ransacked the entire house and kept on shouting and calling the family members all sorts of names. Asha ran towards the Commander and begged him to remove his boots as he was trampling all over the rooms and going towards the small temple. She stopped one of them by grabbing hold of his collar. One of the intruders banged the door of a room and broke it open. Rani woke up. She came out of the room screaming. She started abusing the intruders. She fainted and the kangri slipped through her hands and fell down. The men continued searching the entire house. Asha shouted through the window. The lights went off. Nobody listened. Nobody from the neighbouring houses came out. 'Your husband is on the list. We want him now,' shouted the intruders. In the commotion, the Commander's mask slipped from his face. Asha screamed, 'I have seen you somewhere.' She identified him. He was Hamid. He studied with Vijay. He had dropped out of the school and disappeared. He was rumoured to have gone to Pakistan to become a jihadi.

'We will come again. We won't leave him...'

Bishambar Nath survived. He escaped death. That fateful day he had stayed back at Hogoum. Rahman had caught hold of him and warned him not to go home. Rahman saved him. He gave him another life. Bishambar Nath didn't sleep the entire night. He feared for his family. He was uncertain of their safety. When he reached home, everybody started crying. They thought he had been killed. They didn't know what to do. They sat in silence the entire day. The day ended and evening sank into darkness. The family members hugged one other and huddled in one room. Vijay didn't go to school for a week. The family decided to flee. Bishambar Nath had to get some papers from his office. They packed a few things.

A day before the family was to go away from their village, the killers circled the entire village. They called for Ramesh. Ramesh worked at a chemist shop in the village. Fear engulfed the entire village. Ramesh was abducted from the shop where he worked. His hands were tied and he was blindfolded and taken into a boat. He was kicked and stamped with the butt of a gun leaving his face unrecognisable. His body was scarred with cigarette burns. His eyes were gouged out. The killers dragged him towards a Chinar tree in the village playground. He pleaded for his life and fainted. The killers shot him and then urinated on him. The body was thrown into the river. It was fished out the next morning.

A pall of gloom descended on Bishambar Nath's family. Vyad Kak managed everything for them. He arranged a priest to perform the funeral rites. Rahman got wood from his own house. Asha and Rani sat in the verandah crying and sobbing incessantly. The news of the killing spread across the other villages. Vijay hid in a corner of the room and cried for his brother. Nobody from the village came out. Vijay's friend Rouf attended the funeral. He consoled Vijay. After the funeral pyre was lit, Rouf came close to Vijay and whispered in his ear, 'Vijay, listen to me, these men are on the path of God. They don't kill innocents. They don't kill without reason. Ramesh must have done something wrong. Maybe he was an informer. Don't cry. I pray to God for peace.'

Rouf left. Vijay stood aghast. His legs were trembling. Those words haunted him. The next day, as had been planned earlier, the family left the village. They migrated to a new place and took shelter in a refugee camp. The situation worsened in their village. Their house was set ablaze by unknown persons. Someone broke this news to Bishambar Nath. After this incident, they decided to sell their property to a neighbour who frequented their camp in Jammu. Vijay didn't study further. He hardly talked to anybody. Something disturbed him. He never slept in peace. Rani suffered a stroke. She became bedridden.

Years later, Vijay heard from someone that Rouf's father had been killed by militants. Vijay decided to visit his old village. The family resisted. Vijay carried something in his heart all these years; something that saddened him. He was caught in a torrent of emotion and trauma. He insisted on going. The place he was going to visit was enveloped in violence and bloodshed. One community was working against the other. People were suspicious of one another. Vijay travelled in the night and reached his village the next morning. He went straight to the funeral of Rouf's father. Rouf saw Vijay standing at a distance. People flooded the graveyard. Tears welled up in the eyes of Rouf. He went straight to Vijay and hugged him. He wailed loudly. He said, 'Look Vijay, look what they did to my father?' Vijay threw his arms around Rouf and whispered in his ear, 'Rouf, listen to me, these men are on the path of God. They don't kill innocents. They don't kill without reason. Your father must have done something wrong. Maybe he was an informer. Don't cry. I pray to God for peace.' Rouf was shocked. He stood aghast, fell down on his knees and cried.

Vijay went to the holy pond near the temple, stepped into its cold waters, washed the sacred thread he wore, poured water on his head and later went back to Jammu.

The informers

Deepak Budki

THE city was tense with all sorts of rumours. Those who were suspected to be informers were being hunted down one by one and put to death. For the first time in years, abductions, disappearances and killings had become the order of the day. Fear and anguish were writ large on people's faces. They lost trust in their own shadows. They started to wonder: Do our names appear in the list of informers? Are we on the hit list of militants? Do the militants suspect us of any connection with security forces? Have we been seen talking to any security personnel?

Restlessness swelled in people's hearts and minds. Why should we be singled out for our political leanings? thought some people. But what if we are singled out? What then? People brought out clarificatory notices in the local dailies so that the militants would know that the people who brought out these notices were not connected with any political party.

One does not fear death as much as one fears the very idea of death. Some people tendered unconditional apologies. Some resorted to explaining their positions while others simply fled in horror.

Nilakanth did not take recourse to any of these. He had spent the sixty-five years of his life in Kashmir. Even now he spent his days without fretting about the vitiated atmosphere around him.

The house of Nilakanth, made of old bricks and deodar wood, was situated near a temple on the bank of Jhelum that flowed majestically through Habba Kadal. In the mornings, the sound of temple bells and the call of the muezzin converged. Hawkers thronged the lanes and lured passers-by with their goods. Fisherwomen came out of their houseboats to sell fish. Appetising smells came out of the baker's oven. Fragrance of fresh milk emanated from cowsheds. Hindus recited *shlokas* from *The Gita* and the Muslims read out verses from the *Holy Quran* while buying milk and bread. Horses and mules galloped on the road. Kids rode bicycles. Cows mooed. Dogs barked. Boys and girls marched towards school.

But that day something was amiss. Nilakanth was lost in deep thought. His wife had cleaned the pipe of his hookah and changed its water. Nilakanth filled the *chilam* with tobacco, placed burning coals in the coal container, and then took long drags. While exhaling, clouds of smoke came out of his mouth. He coughed for a while and then lost himself in a reverie.

He remembered the day of his marriage when he had to cross the Habba Kadal Bridge since Arundati's house was situated on the other side of the river. He could see her parental house from his own window, and watch her standing by the window. The majestic Jhelum separated their houses.

After finishing her daily chores, Arundati sat by his side. 'One doesn't realise how time flies. Forty-five years have passed since we got married,' Nilakanth said to her looking at her in disbelief.

'You sound nostalgic today.' Arundati was pleasantly surprised.

'Do you know what date it is today?'

'I don't. Why? Our life is like a caravan of lost days and nights. Had there been no picture of God on the calendar, we would have thrown it away long back.' Arundati squinted at the calendar nailed on the wall.

'You are right, Arni.'

Arni remembered that she had kept tea to boil on the heater.

'Arni, do you remember how I used to ogle at you for hours from the roof of my house?'

'What has possessed you today?'

She interrupted her husband but later became nostalgic about her childhood. She was five years younger than her husband but due to acute arthritis her feet had swollen. She had no one to help her carry out the domestic chores. She did everything all by herself. Her son was in America and her daughter lived in Bombay.

'My right eyelid has been trembling for the last so many days. God knows what is to befall us.' Arundati tore a small piece of paper, moistened it with her saliva and then placed it on her right eyelid in order to stop the trembling.

'Our destiny is written in the Heavens. Whatever has to happen will definitely happen.' Nilakanth sounded pensive and resigned.

Arundati had never seen her husband resigned to fate earlier. She showed her annoyance when she couldn't get replies to her queries. For the last several days she had observed Nilakanth fretting over something. At night, Nilakanth would remain awake for hours and peep through the cracks in the window into the darkness outside.

'There is so much anxiety on your face. What is keeping you awake at nights? Have faith in God. Everything will be all right.' Arundati would console her husband.

'Arni, it is not anxiety but you should know that the situation has taken a bloody turn. Only Lord Shiva knows what is going to happen next.' He laid bare the facts before his wife.

Arundati remembered the time when the tribals from Pakistan invaded the valley. She was eighteen at the time. The memory of killings and rape and arson still sent shivers down her spine. The bloodthirsty invaders had killed thousands of innocent people in Uri and Baramulla. They had not even spared the nuns of a local convent. Many women and young girls had committed suicide to save their honour. Darkness had descended upon Kashmir.

Arundati had shown unbounded courage those days. To this day she was proud of herself. But now a similar situation loomed. 'Why do you worry? We have been through hell during the tribal raid. We should face this ordeal with courage,' she said to her husband.

Having heard his wife's reassuring words, Nilakanth heaved a sigh of relief but at the same time he pitied Arundati's innocence and simplicity.

As days went by, Nilakanth's worries multiplied. The news of killings and abductions terrified him. His wife regretted not having listened to the pleas of her children.

'This is all our fault,' she sighed. 'Veeru had invited us to America so many times but you refused to go. God only knows what keeps you glued to this place. Agreed that Veeru's wife is an American but how does it matter. She would not throw us out of our son's house. We would just occupy a corner there. We could have looked after our grandchildren. Children are the biggest source of satisfaction to old people like us.' Arundati spoke her heart out.

'It is not about Veeru's wife. You don't understand. At this age one is afraid to leave one's home. All our lives we have not even gone beyond Jawahar Tunnel. How can we think of leaving our home and staying in a foreign country? Who knows what kind of a country America is? What kind of people live there? Why do you put all the blame on me? Your heart, too, is not inclined to leave our nest.'

'Okay, leave Veeru aside. Kaki, too, had invited us to stay at her place in Bombay. You refused to go there because you thought staying at a daughter's house is a sin.'

'Arni, you just don't understand. If our children really loved us they would have come here and taken us with them. But they don't care. Their invitations are...'

'Both of them were ready to come but they are afraid of you. Your decisions are final. Remember, you had written letters to them not to come here.'

'Today is the 7th day of Shrawan. It is the birthday of Veeru's son. You should have prepared some delicacies today.'

'It is Janmashtami today. Kaki's daughter too was born today. I hope you sent them a telegram? It isn't too late to ask Veeru to send us tickets. What do you think? Will you write a letter to him and tell him we are ready to go to America.'

'I am also thinking on similar lines. We should go to Bombay for a few days and then go to America from there.'

'Do whatever you think is right. But please hurry. We may not have much time left.'

At night, Nilakanth was uneasy. He couldn't sleep well. He got up several times to check if all windows and doors were bolted properly. He paced up and down the room. Sleep eluded him. He kept turning in his bed. Suddenly, there was loud knocking on the main door. The couple froze. Nilakanth didn't know what to do. His wife prayed. The couple heard the sound of the door being forced open. Moments later, two young men with mufflers over their faces and with pistols in their hands entered the room.

Next day, newspapers carried the headline: *Mujahids kill two informers in Habba Kadal.*

(Translated from Urdu by the author)

The world cup

Adarsh Ajit

I was walking through the market of my village to meet my Muslim friends and to chat with them. I saw my favourite teacher, tall, well-built and handsome walking on the opposite side. Kashmir was peaceful those days.

No trouble. No violence. No sloganeering.

I greeted my teacher. '*Adaab*!'

'*Adaab*. How are you? How is your father?'

'All well, sir.'

'I am writing a letter to the Prime Minister of India.'

I did not understand what my teacher wanted to say.

I replied, 'Okay, sir.'

'Have you heard the news on the radio?'

'No, sir.'

The teacher looked angry. His face was red.

He continued, 'Is this a war? Is this a way to broadcast the news?'

I still did not get what he wanted to say. I simply asked, 'Sir, I do not understand. What news? What letter? Why a letter to the Prime Minister?'

'Azlaan Shah Hockey tournament final was played between India and Pakistan. India won by one goal. But the radio carried the news as: *Aakhir kaar Hindustaan ne Pakistaan se badla le hi liya* (After all, India took its revenge against Pakistan).

'O, yes sir. I understand now. Yes, I heard the news.'

'Tell me, is this the way to inform people about the result of a match?'

I kept mum.

'I am going to write a letter.'

I was analysing my teacher's words. For me he was an Indian. But it was shocking that he felt hurt by the tone of the news broadcast on the radio.

When I met the friends who were waiting for me in an apple orchard, I saw anger on their faces too. I asked them, 'Why is your mood off today?'

'Because we lost the match.'

'Matches are matches.' I plucked an apple from a tree and began to eat it.

'India has no culture,' they said.

'I do not understand,' I said.

'The news they broadcast was in bad taste,' they said.

I kept mum. I understood that the way the news had been read was not received well.

We deviated from the topic. We went about our ways and promised to meet the following Sunday to watch a film on TV in the school premises.

THE hockey world cup final was being played between India and Pakistan. All the Kashmiri Muslim youth had transistors in their hands. Pandits were listening to the commentary in their homes. The match was interesting. Sometimes it was going Pakistan's way and sometimes India's. When it was going Pakistan's way crackers were burst and when it went India's way there was a mourning-like situation. Pandits did not express their joy by bursting crackers. Only two minutes were left for the match when the Indian players in a bid to score a goal were awarded a penalty strike. Muslims wore mournful looks. Pandits were happy but did not express their feelings openly. It was really a war-like situation. Suddenly, Jasdev Singh the commentator shouted: *Aur yeh goal.*

India won the World Cup and sadness prevailed everywhere in the Muslim households in Kashmir. Some commented that it was not a goal because the ball struck the goal post first and then entered into the goal. They were giving many explanations. Pandits remained indoors to avoid estrangement on the issue. But Indian TV started showing the same match almost daily. We did not go to watch the film in the school out of fear. We were fans of Bollywood movies those days. The government had installed TV at two places. We went to watch the movie another day. When there was a commercial break during the movie the match was again telecast. It was good for us but bad for Muslims. We wanted to watch this match on the TV.

We were watching the match though all the Muslims were abusing India. They went on saying that the goal was controversial and, as such, this match should have been played again. We were accustomed to facing such incidents in Kashmir.

We had a peculiar approach to avoid any quarrel and conflict under such circumstances. When the time came when we could have seen how India scored the maiden goal against Pakistan, I saw an educated man, who was serving in All India Radio, climb the electric pole. He reached the top of the pole. He twisted the main wire many times with his bare hands. And it did not take him long to cut the wire. Electricity went off. The TV screen went blank. And we did not watch that goal. No Muslim said anything to that man. Pandits could not say anything. Such was the anti-India sentiment of the Muslims of our village. This man later became a hero. We stayed calm and cool for an hour or so. Then another young Muslim, who was my class fellow, also climbed that electric pole and connected the wires. The TV came on and the film resumed. We watched the film.

All our lives we had seen such activities when there was a match between India and Pakistan. If Pakistan won, Muslims were jubilant. If India won they became gloomy.

The last rites

Rajesh Kaul

MY name is Kashi Nath, but I am called Kakini. It does not seem to be true or believable. But it is the truth. From the beginning, my family and even outsiders called me Kakini. It became my nickname. But, by and by, they lost interest in it and I got accustomed to this name. If I would not hear the call 'Kakini' two or three times a day, I would feel something missing, as if something had been left incomplete. Well, I am responsible for this. Though I am old enough to have retired from service, yet I don't do anything without the approval or consent of Kakini. Only after consulting her do I attend to the daily tasks. Even such a trifling activity as buying vegetables calls for Kakini's approval. She, too, got used to this phenomenon. She wanted me to be near her, seek her advice, and consult her. That would keep her contented.

Again, if I say the truth, you may not believe me. Kakini was not my real mother who gave birth to me. But I treated her as though she was my real mother. Early in the morning, I would bring her a cup of Kahwah with cinnamon and a fresh loaf of bread. I would feed her myself, and only after she had had her tea, I would do my morning chores. At night, I would make her bed and even chant a hymn to lull her to sleep. She slept like a child. Having recently retired, I had enough time to do all the work at home, giving her no chance to feel any discomfort. Whatever she asked for, I would provide, even though sometimes it would be difficult. Aging had taken its toll; her speech had been adversely affected and sometimes she would lose her balance of mind, too. Even though I was fully conscious of her condition, I gave her no indication that I found something amiss in her condition. Maybe I was not prepared to believe that she would grow old and experience health issues.

One day, instead of calling me by my name Kashi Nath, she shouted, 'Kakini'. It was in such a natural tone that my wife Usha could not at once understand whether I was calling her or that she had called me by the same nickname. It was her voice, though the tone resembled mine. My wife could have lost her composure, because of this habit of mine—of consulting Kakini on every matter. In the beginning, she did show irritation. She felt vexed. But gradually she became used to it. Upon hearing the call, I rushed to mother's room. I was stunned and bewildered. She had fallen off the bed. Instinctively, I blurted out, 'O Goddess Sharika, have mercy.' Hearing me scream, Usha barged into the room in panic. Both of us lifted Kakini up and dashed to the doctor's clinic.

I don't know whether it was the clinic that cast a spell or something else. But something happened that day. Usha accompanied her to the doctors' room, while I waited outside. Sitting on the bench, I relapsed into the past. I stood in the presence of my real mother. I could recognise her from a distance. Her headgear had a bright ribbon band with a cape-like covering. A moon-shaped tilak, made out of saffron paste, shone on her forehead. She wore a pheran with a waistband that was made of pashmina. My mother's name was Lacchkuj. She was at work in the kitchen garden. I had come home and had brought some money. I called her from a distance. 'Kakini,' I screamed. Hearing my call, she dropped the tool, jumped over the low wooden fence and came near me. For sometime, she had been asking me to get her a green-coloured shawl. She snatched the bag I held in my hand and took out the gift I had brought for her. She was ecstatic.

That shawl stood her in good stead, when terrorists showered bullets on my father. Kakini used it as a bandage to stop the bleeding, but my father had breathed his last before we could do anything. I don't cry. But you can't stop tears. Somehow, we got us a truck and fled from the place, along with the ashes of my father. Kakini was not used to the heat and high temperatures. Staying outside the temple complex on a footpath in scorching heat pained her. But she didn't complain. I would buy ice blocks and rub them on her soles. Her voice became feeble. Her health worsened. I could not really give her much comfort or serve her properly. I would step outside at daybreak to join a queue for the registration of the displaced, and return only at dusk, almost half-dead. We had to get ourselves registered as migrants and for that we had to provide proof of having fled our homes. At the registration counter, we had to wait for our turn.

The queues were endless. It took days for my turn to come. Everyday was a nightmare. Our struggles were unending. Some people would come and talk to us while we waited endlessly in long queues. They would offer words of comfort. Their assurances were hollow. During this difficult time, my mother died. There was no great fuss about it, no great mourning. I feel responsible for her death. She died because of me. She died away from her home. She died in exile. I could not bear her passing. After her death, I would go to Gita Bhawan everyday to visit the spot where Kakini had waited for her turn to be given a ration card. The spot where she had waited and waited till she could hold no more! I quietly placed flowers at the spot. The thought perturbs me. If only I had stood in her place, she would not have died out of exhaustion. But the authorities at Gita Bhawan would have never allowed me to fill in for her. The hunt for a ration card became the cause of Kakini's death.

When I saw a middle-aged woman wearing the same kind of *taranga* (headgear) with the same green waistband, I felt as if Kakini had come back to life. I felt as if God had answered my prayer. I thought I would lighten my burden by talking to her and comforting her. But she did not wait for me to say anything. As soon as she saw me, she said, 'Are you Lakshmi Nath?' Hearing this, I could perceive that she had met with a greater tragedy. There was pain and hope in her voice. The staff at the temple confirmed my suspicion. 'She calls everybody Lakshmi Nath,' they said. 'She has been here for three days. Three days ago, her son left her here. He hasn't returned since then. Don't know what sort of allurements he used to persuade her to wait here endlessly. She is waiting for her son to take her back. But so far nobody has come. Neither her son nor her relatives! So she mistakes everybody for her son, Lakshmi Nath.'

I remembered my mother. I believed this was a godsent opportunity to do all the things that I could not do for my own mother. I brought the woman to the rented place we had taken shelter in. I thought my wife would throw a fit. But she did not. She began to look after the old woman, thinking that it might help me in overcoming my grief and misery.

When Kakini came out of the doctor's room, my dream ended. I was preparing to meet the doctor when he gestured at me to accompany him to his room. 'Are you her son?' he asked.

Kakini, I screamed. The doctor stared at me for sometime and began offering words of comfort. 'One should not lose hope as long as one breathes,' he said to me. The doctor said it in a very cordial manner so as to cheer me up.

When I reached home, I resolved to search for Kakini's real family. My wife and I served her, day after day. But after a few days, she too passed away. I got an obituary published in the newspapers, hoping that her family would see her photograph and come for the last rites. But no one came. Ultimately, I decided to perform the last rites myself. On the tenth day, the rites were to be performed on the bank of a river. All my relatives came for the ritual. A barber gave me a tonsure as per the Hindu customs. That very moment, on the other side of the river, a man who seemed my age was also receiving a tonsure. But he was alone. There was nobody with him. Moments later, I saw him performing the last rites of someone.

(Translated from Kashmiri by J L Raina)

Father and son

Rinku Koul

DWARIKA Nath was relieved of the responsibility of marrying off his daughter three years ago. Now he wanted to marry off his son, Ravi. After the death of his wife, he lived alone most of the time. He was happy when his children were around. Ravi was very eager to go to Pune to pursue a degree in engineering.

I would see Dwarika Nath at the milkman's shop every morning.

One day he said, 'Ravi has completed his engineering and has joined a private company. Now I want him to get married. Please look for a suitable girl.'

Listening to him, I joked, 'It is possible your son has got married there, and may be having a child too.'

Laughing he said, 'I have told Ravi one thing repeatedly that he is free to do whatever he wants, but the girl he wants to marry should be from our own community.'

Dwarika Nath and his daughter Meena were looking for a suitable bride for Ravi. They finally selected a girl. After obtaining the consent of the boy and the girl, the engagement took place; the ring ceremony was performed and the date of marriage was fixed.

Ravi came from Pune a few days before the wedding. Dwarika Nath and his son-in-law had made all the arrangements. The marriage ceremony was held as scheduled. Dwarika Nath was very happy and relaxed. Within a week or so, Ravi and his wife left for Pune. Dwarika Nath was alone again but he was satisfied that as a father he had fulfilled his responsibilities during his lifetime.

The days went by. Dwarika Nath developed a keen desire of having a grandchild with whom he would play. This desire was also fulfilled when Ravi informed him one day on telephone, 'Daddy, you have become a grandfather.' This brought a lot of happiness to Dwarika Nath. He wanted to visit Pune immediately but his failing health did not allow him to undertake the journey. He kept on asking Ravi to pay a short visit to him so that he could see the grandchild and fondle him in his lap. Ravi would always say that he was hard pressed for time and that it would not be easy for him to visit his father.

Dwarika Nath's health was failing day-by-day.

One day, he thought, One cannot trust one's life. I may die any time. Who knows if anyone will be around when I breathe my last! There may be no one to put even a drop of water in my mouth. Ravi may not be able to perform my last rites and rituals.

Dwarika Nath talked to his family priest and asked him to perform all the rituals for him in his lifetime. The priest readily came forward to perform all the rituals that are normally performed after the death.

Dwarika Nath passed away after a few days. On hearing the news of his death, I immediately rushed to his place. His body had been kept on the floor. His daughter was crying and wailing loudly, 'My beloved father, how nice you have been to us! You have fulfilled all the needs of my brother and me. Our mother died in our childhood and you did not let her absence impact us. But your own children could not be with you when you needed them the most. They did not even put a spoonful of water in your mouth.'

I asked Dwarika Nath's son-in-law, 'Have you informed Ravi?'

'Yes, we have. He has his own problems. He has to get permission from his Company, and arrange for railway tickets. We cannot wait for his arrival. We don't have to get anything because his father-in-law has already brought all the items required for the cremation and other rituals.'

Ravi along with his wife and child arrived after three days.

(Translated from Kashmiri by Omkar Nath Koul)

About the Editors

Arvind Gigoo taught English Literature in various colleges in the Jammu and Kashmir state. He is the author of three books, including, most recently, *Gulliver In Kashmir*. He translates Kashmiri poems and short stories into English. His writings are published in several newspapers and literary journals.

Siddhartha Gigoo is the author of *The Garden of Solitude*, *A Fistful of Earth and Other Stories* and *Mehr*. His short story *The Umbrella Man* won the Commonwealth Short Story Prize 2015 for Asia. His two short films *The Last Day* and *Goodbye, Mayfly* have won several awards at international film festivals. He also co-edited *A Long Dream of Home (The Persecution, Exodus and Exile of Kashmiri Pandits)*. Siddhartha's writings appear in several literary journals. To know more about him, visit siddharthagigoo.com

Adarsh Ajit is a columnist, reviewer and translator. He is the author of a book of Urdu poems *Yaad jo aatay hain voh din*. His write-ups on literary, social and political issues are published in various literary journals and newspapers. These days, he's working on his debut novel.

Contributors

Agnishekhar, a poet, short story writer and researcher, has authored six books in Hindi. He is an activist and convener of Panun Kashmir.

Autar Krishan Rahbar is the author of *A History of Kashmiri Literature* (in Kashmiri). He writes short stories and radio dramas in Kashmiri.

Chandrakanta, author of more than twenty books in Hindi, is the recipient of several literary awards such as Vyas Samaan (K K Birla Foundation), Jammu and Kashmir Cultural Academy Award, Kalpana Chawla Excellence Award for excellence in Hindi Literature, Richa Samman for Hindi Literature, Hindi Academy, Haryana Sahitya Akademi and Chandrawati Shukla Puraskar. *A Street in Srinagar,* the English translation of her Hindi novel *Ailan Gali Zinda Hai* was shortlisted for the 2012 DSC Prize for South Asian Literature. *The Saga Of Satisar* has been longlisted for the 2018 DSC Prize for South Asian Literature.

Deepak Budki, a former Chief Post Master General (J&K Circle), has published nine collections of short stories in Urdu and three collections of critical essays. He lives in Jammu.

Harikrishna Kaul wrote stories in Hindi and Kashmiri. He was bestowed with the Jammu and Kashmir Academy of Art, Culture and Languages award.

Henna Koul is an occasional writer. She teaches English at a school in New Delhi.

Kirti Kaul worked in the Media Industry for more than ten years, including a four-year stint with the *National Geographic Channel*, India. She's also worked with Teri Press and Intach where she wrote and edited books for children. At present, she is working as a Research and Resources Facilitator with the Shiv Nadar School, Noida.

Kishni Pandita taught English Literature in various schools in Kashmir and Shillong. Her stories have appeared in *Women's Era*. She has written stories and short plays for the All India Radio's North East Service. *The Last Exodus* is her debut book of short stories.

Kundan Lal Chowdhury is a physician, poet and writer. He is the author of *Of Gods, Men and Militants*, *A Thousand-Petalled Garland and Other Poems*, *Enchanting World of Infants*, *Faith and Frenzy* and *Why Don't You Convert?* His book, *Enchanting World of Infants,* was conferred the Best Book Award for Excellence in Literature by the J&K Academy of Arts, Culture and Languages.

Khema Kaul is the author of *Samay key baad (meri diary)*, *Baadalon mein aag* (poetry), *Dardpur* and *Nikki tawi par rehearsal* (novels in Hindi).

Khushboo Mattoo is an occasional poet and works for a private FM channel in Jammu.

Maharaj Krishen Santoshi has authored five books in Hindi.

Moti Lal Kemmu has written twelve plays in Kashmiri, one in Hindi, a novel in Hindi and a book on folk theatre and culture of Kashmir in Kashmiri. He is the recipient of the Sahitya Akademi Award, Sangeet Natak Akademi Award, Harmony Award, and the Padma Shree.

Monika Ajay Kaul is a poet and painter. She teaches brand marketing at a college in Noida.

Neeraj Santoshi is an author and journalist.

Nipa Chiragi is a journalist with *Mint*.

Pushkar Nath Dhar is the author of a book of essays *Chetinaav*.

Parmarth Gupta writes short stories and essays. His debut novel is published on *Wattpad*, an online platform.

Pratush Koul studies at a college in Haryana. He writes short stories, poems and articles.

Rajesh Kaul worked for Doordarshan Kendra in Jullundur. He writes short stories in Kashmiri.

Rinku Koul has written a book of short stories in Kashmiri.

Subhash Kak is the Regents Professor and Head of Computer Science Department at Oklahoma State University in Stillwater. He is notable for his publications on history, Indology, the philosophy of science, ancient astronomy, and the history of mathematics. In 2018, he was appointed member of Indian Prime

Minister's Science, Technology and Innovation Advisory Council.

Shilpa Raina is a journalist and writes on visual arts and culture. She has previously worked with *IANS* and *Deccan Herald*. She has written for *The Hindu*, *The Indian Express* and *Discover India*. These days, she's working with *CNN-News18*.

Seema Bhat is an entrepreneur and a photographer.

Sushant Dhar is a writer and singer. His essays and short stories have appeared in various literary journals in India.

Tej Nath Dhar has authored *History-Fiction Interface in Indian English Novel* and *Under the Shadow of Militancy: The Diary of an Unknown Kashmiri*. His critical essays and writings appear in several journals in India and abroad.

Varad Sharma is the co-editor of *A Long Dream of Home: The Persecution, Exodus and Exile of Kashmiri Pandits*. His writings have appeared in several magazines and newspapers. These days, he's working on his memoir of growing up in exile.

Translators

C L Hakhoo is a novelist, short story writer and translator. He retired as Director, Doordarshan, Jullundur.

J L Raina is a writer and translator.

Omkar Nath Koul is a writer and translator.

P L Waguzari is a writer and translator.

Ranjana Kaul is Associate Professor of English at the College of Vocational Studies, Delhi University. Her articles, reviews and English translations of Kashmiri and Hindi short stories are published in various literary journals including *Indian Literature, New Horizon* and *Hindi.*

Sualeh Keen is a graphic artist, cultural critic, writer and translator.

Tej K Zadoo, a retired professor of Physics, has translated Shaiva texts *Parapraveshika* into English and *Pratibhignya Hridyam* into Hindi. His research papers appear in several scientific journals.